WE'RE
SPEAKING

WE'RE SPEAKING

THE LIFE LESSONS OF KAMALA HARRIS:
HOW TO USE YOUR VOICE,
BE ASSERTIVE, AND OWN YOUR STORY

HITHA PALEPU

LITTLE, BROWN SPARK

New York   Boston   London

Little, Brown Spark
Hachette Book Group
1290 Avenue of the Americas, New York, NY 10104
littlebrownspark.com

First Edition: October 2021

Little Brown Spark is an imprint of Little, Brown and Company, a division of Hachette Book Group, Inc. The Little, Brown Spark name and logo are trademarks of Hachette Book Group, Inc.

The publisher is not responsible for websites (or their content) that are not owned by the publisher.

The Hachette Speakers Bureau provides a wide range of authors for speaking events. To find out more, go to hachettespeakersbureau.com or call (866) 376-6591.

Library of Congress Control Number: 2021939754

Printing 1, 2021

ISBN 978-0-316-28290-1

LSC-C

Printed in the United States of America

To the ones that eat no *for breakfast, speak their truth,
and always show up excellent.*

Contents

WE'RE
SPEAKING

Preface

January 21, 2021, was a bitterly cold night, even under the glare of the studio lights. Kamala Devi Harris, clad in a black dress, tuxedo overcoat, and leather gloves, stood on the steps of the Lincoln Memorial. She took a deep breath, pressed her shoulders back, and put her chin up. With a smile, she delivered her first words to the world as the forty-ninth vice president of the United States.

"We are undaunted in our belief that we shall overcome—that we will rise up. This is American aspiration. In the middle of the Civil War, Abraham Lincoln saw a better future and built it with land grant colleges and the transcontinental railroad. In the middle of the civil rights movement, Dr. King fought for racial justice and economic justice. American aspiration is what drove the women of this nation throughout history to demand equal rights and the authors of the Bill of Rights to claim freedoms that had rarely been written down before. A great experiment takes great determination, the will to do the work, and then the wisdom to keep refining, keep tinkering, keep perfecting. The same determination is being realized in America today."

That same determination, will, wisdom, and aspiration had been realized earlier that day, as Kamala Harris was sworn in as the country's first woman vice president, and also the first Black and South Asian vice president.

In the months that Kamala Harris went from being the junior senator from California to vice president of the United States, I asked hundreds of women what she meant to them, and the answers were incredibly varied. *Hope, representation, strength,* and *courage* were some of the most common answers, as was *shattering the glass ceiling.* Others commented on how she's evolved on issues, publicly and openly. For Black women, who have been the backbone of our democracy, they felt ownership — especially in the "we" when she called President-Elect Biden and said, "We did it, Joe." For South Asians, it was feeling a deeper belonging to America as she recognized her *chithi*s (her mother's sisters) in her acceptance speech. For blended and multicultural families, it was a shattering of stereotypes that had been the norm in media and culture. And for children, it showed that anyone could be elected to one of the most formidable and prestigious positions in the world. Girls saw themselves as powerful, and boys saw that power belonged to women as much as men.

As for me? I felt a lot of feelings.

As a longtime fan of Kamala Harris, I felt elated as I watched the inauguration ceremony. I felt pride — as a woman, as a South Asian, and as an American. I felt hope, which I hadn't felt much of in the past five years. I felt a sense of relief that our vice president's purpose in life was, and is, to make our country better for everyone. Most of all, I felt seen. I felt seen by Kamala, a woman who leads with ambition and is devoted to her family in equal measure. I felt seen because of all these things I've listed, and many more.

I first heard of Kamala Harris when she was attorney general of California. I was working for SciDose, an early-stage pharmaceutical company. I had just stepped into a business development role that had me at the negotiating table quite a bit. The job also had me traveling constantly, which became the basis for my blog,

"Hitha on the Go." I kept CNN on in the background whenever I was unpacking, repacking, and getting ready in the many hotel rooms I lived in.

On a random February day in a random hotel in 2012, one story captured my attention as I caught up on emails. California had secured an $18 billion settlement for relief from the subprime mortgage crisis, which was negotiated by the state's attorney general. I remember my hands freezing on my keyboard, my full attention on the television screen. The report mentioned Kamala Harris's rejection of the lenders' initial offer as one of her first acts as AG, and the months of negotiations that led to this announcement. Harris appeared on the screen, in her trademark pantsuit and pearls. "Well, I'll tell you there's a simple principle in law and, in particular, contract law, which is the deal ain't done just based on a promise. It's based on a promise, and acceptance, and then performance."

My fingers quickly flew across my keyboard attempting to capture the quote, which I've revisited often in my work. Negotiating deals is a large part of my career, from licensing agreements with other pharmaceutical companies to brand campaigns to investments in start-ups. Getting a signature on the contract is not the end goal, but merely the beginning of a partnership. This quote reminds me to build consensus (acceptance) and over-deliver on my end (performance). After hearing this quote, I spent the next few hours researching Kamala Harris, reading every interview and watching every video I could about her. For the first time in a long time, I could see myself being like Kamala, in a position of power that I wanted to earn one day.

Being a woman—a young woman of color at that—continues to be the exception in the pharmaceutical industry. I had a number of mentors and sponsors who invested their time and support in me, but I felt uncomfortable asking them what I should wear for a certain meeting, how to approach the push/pull of a negotiation, and how to speak in a room filled with men so they listen. In Kamala Harris, I had a model that showed me how to communicate, negotiate, and show up in the rooms I still felt uncomfortable in. I jotted down quotes, took notes on her style, and created a digital notebook of "Kamala-isms" that I could refer to when I needed. She became a mentor from afar, and I actively kept up with her. Kamala Harris helped me step into and own my power in every professional role I've held: pharmaceutical executive, tech entrepreneur, content creator, and author.

Kamala's childhood—and her mother's story—also

helped me feel a greater sense of belonging to these United States of America. Both Kamala's mother, Shyamala Gopalan Harris, and my father's elder brother, Ram Palepu, came to the United States before the Immigration and Nationality Act was passed in 1965, when only one hundred Indians were granted visas every year. Shyamala raised her daughters alone with a deep sense of civic duty, much how my aunt Shanti Palepu Veluri (my father's elder sister) raised my cousin Bob (named after Robert Kennedy). Bob grew up to attend the Naval Academy and serve as a lieutenant in the US Navy. Shyamala's career mirrored that of Nagesh Palepu, my father, who also held numerous research jobs and seized every new opportunity that came his way. In both private and public research settings, the bar for advancement was set impossibly high for people of color. Both of them remained laser focused on their North Stars: Shyamala's to cure cancer, my father's to develop the best medicines possible. Shyamala also reminds me of my mother, in making the mundane magical and encouraging me to dream big and work harder. My mother approached every move precipitated by my father's job with a sense of adventure, and the way she quickly packed and unpacked our homes was nothing short of witchcraft. "Go win the world," she told me often. "But at home, I'm the boss. So go do what I told you to do."

My life has come full circle from the first time I spotted Kamala Harris on television. Today, I run Rhoshan Pharmaceuticals alongside my father. I invest in early-stage companies that are founded by and focused on women, and I serve on two nonprofit boards. I've moved away from my travel blog, but continue to create content online with my #5SmartReads newsletter and my Instagram account. I speak frequently on entrepreneurship, investing, and the motherhood–work juggle. I am a proud wife and mother, and raising our sons to be supportive, strong, feminist men is the most important job I will ever have.

Kamala Harris has helped me own every single one of these roles with grace, confidence, and certainty of my own power. I am deeply honored to write this book and share her story in the context of helping you to do the same.

This is not a book that will magically transform you into Kamala Harris, though I hope you learn new things about her and the people who helped raise, inspire, and support her. I hope this book will help you be braver, stronger, kinder, more confident, and ready to claim your power. I hope you highlight the sections that speak to you, and bookmark the pages you find helpful. I hope you return to this book when you're feeling low, lost, hurt, or hopeless. I hope it brings you inspiration and guidance, and helps you get back on track of the amazing life you're creating.

Shoulders back. Chin up. Deep breath.

We're speaking.

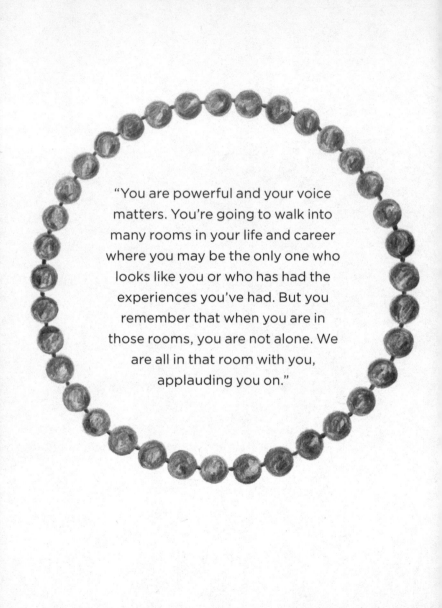

"You are powerful and your voice matters. You're going to walk into many rooms in your life and career where you may be the only one who looks like you or who has had the experiences you've had. But you remember that when you are in those rooms, you are not alone. We are all in that room with you, applauding you on."

CHAPTER 1

Your Name and Your Multitudes Are Your Power

KA-ma-la, Ka-MA-la, Ka-MA-la-MA-la-MA-la, I don't know, whatever."

Senator David Perdue had joined President Trump for a rally, and on a sunny October day, stood on a platform warming up the crowd and purposely dismissing and poking fun at the soon-to-be history-making, glass ceiling–breaking vice president's first name. The name of a woman who happened to be one of his colleagues.

For Kamala Harris, the incident was a common one. She had lived a lifetime of her name being mispronounced and mocked, and this was neither the first nor the last time this would happen to her. The reaction this time, however, was different. #MyNameIs quickly began to trend on Twitter, with celebrities and individuals sharing the meanings of their name and their heritage. For those with non-anglicized names, it was an opportunity to reclaim the power of their names after countless experiences of mispronunciation, mocking, or careless nicknames.

#MyNameIs Meenakshi. I'm named after the Hindu goddess, as well as my great great grandmother. I come from a long line of strong women who taught me to be proud of my heritage and to demand respect—especially from racist white men like @sendavidperdue who are threatened by us. @meena—Meena Harris, founder of Phenomenal and niece of Vice President Harris

#MyNameIs Mayra. And yes, I'm constantly correcting people on how to say it. But I carry it proudly as a reminder of my Mexican culture. I used to hesitate to correct ppl, but my parents did not traverse miles and cross a border for me not to stand up for myself. @lachicamayra—Mayra Macías, executive director of Latino Victory

#MyNameIs Malcolm Kenyatta. My father named me to honor the legacy of two giants in the Black diaspora: Malcolm X and Jomo Kenyatta. @

sendavidperdue might not care, but my name reminds me every day the systems of discrimination we must uproot. @malcolmkenyatta—Malcolm Kenyatta, Pennsylvania state senator

#MyNameIs Zara. My parents spent a lot of time and energy picking out a name that would be easily pronounceable for non-Indian people. But they shouldn't have had to do that. It shouldn't be on POC to shave off pieces of our culture to make life easier for white people. @ZarainDC—Zara Ahmed, US international policy officer for Guttmacher Institute

OWN THE POWER OF YOUR NAME

Kamala Devi Harris has always known the power of a name. Kamala means "lotus" in Sanskrit, and is another name for Lakshmi, the Hindu goddess of wealth and prosperity. Devi is the Sanskrit word for *goddess*, but is also attributed to the Hindu mother goddess. "A culture that worships goddesses produces strong women," said Shyamala Gopalan Harris. Naming her daughters Kamala Devi and Maya Lakshmi (Maya is another name for the Hindu goddess Durga) was a way to preserve their Indian identity. Their names also foreshadowed the kind of women they would grow up to be.

Kamala speaks about names reverently, remarking that a name is the first gift children are given from their family. Names represent both the history and the future of the family, and are given with love. If you are ever lucky enough to meet Kamala Harris, she will ask for your full name and will make sure she pronounces it correctly. Learning someone's name and pronouncing it correctly is a dignity owed to all of us, no matter how unfamiliar our name may be to someone else.

It takes some time and growth to step into your name's power. For me, it took a solid fifteen years. My full name is Hitha Nagini Palepu (pronounced HIT-the NAAg-ee-nee PAAL-uh-poo). Growing up in the '90s with darker skin and a last name that ended in -*pu* was a social death sentence. "Pale-poo-poo" and "Pale-poop" were familiar taunts from classmates, and one enterprising child used my full name to dub me "Hit the Pile of Poop." I dismissed the comments and ignored the taunts in school, but would return home in tears and boldly declare I was changing my name.

Despite my attempts to change my first name to Jennifer or adopt Bharathy (my mother's name) as my last name, my parents wiped my tears, delivered tight hugs filled with love, and reminded me of the power of my name. "Hitha means 'good' in Sanskrit. You are good— you have a good heart, and you will do many good things," my mother would whisper in my ear, while smoothing down my hair and rubbing my back. "Nagini means 'queen of the cobras.' She is strong and powerful. It is the feminine version of my name [Nagesh], and I am proud to share the name with you," my dad would repeat to me on our Saturday trips to his office.

As time passed, the taunts stopped but the mispronunciations remained. Rarely were they ill-intentioned, but every mispronunciation tore me up a little bit. At my graduation from the University of Washington, I was one of three students chosen to address the tens of thousands gathered at Husky Stadium, as co-chair of the senior class gift. My fellow speakers' names were introduced clearly and correctly. I was introduced as "Hi-thu Poo-laa-poo." I grinned, made my remarks and introduced the husky statue that would be installed by the student union building, and took my seat. But inside, I was seething.

Each of these slights, from minor ones in a new class to one made in a full football stadium, tore up my heart a little bit. But those tears healed into a stronger muscle that has helped me occupy spaces and roles that were not built for people like me, and to hold them with strength, grace, and the respect I want for myself.

My experiences are all too familiar for those with non-white names. But the impact goes far beyond our personal experiences. Constant mispronunciations or callous dismissal of someone's name is a racial micro-aggression, with significant impact on mental health.

A 2012 study published in *Race Ethnicity and Education* examined the impact of racial microaggressions on K–12 students. The data showed that these microaggressions negatively impacted the emotional well-being of students of color. "The racist practice of mispronouncing names has evolved from a long history of changing people of color's names to strip them of their dignity and humanity," Rita Kohli, the author of the study, told RadioActive.

The burden of name pronunciation typically falls on the people with unique names, which needs to change. "Learning to pronounce a colleague's name correctly is not just a common courtesy but it's an important effort in creating an inclusive workplace, one that emphasizes psychological safety and belonging," says Ruchika Tulshyan. Asking "How do I pronounce your name?" is not a sign of weakness or ignorance. Rather, it's a sign of esteem and tells that person, "I see you. I honor you. I respect you." It is worth the extra time to ask for a proper pronunciation and to say a name correctly—even if it takes a few tries—before continuing the conversation. Instead of backtracking a mispronunciation with "I've never heard that name before," just ask them how to pronounce it before you attempt to say it.

Repeating the person's name throughout the conversation will help you master the pronunciation as well as remember it, which is something we all too often forget. If you're reintroduced to someone, say, "Remind me of your name again." If you're newly aware that you've been mispronouncing someone's name for some time, do something about it. Apologize, ask for clarification, and commit to mastering it.

It can feel uncomfortable or embarrassing to ask someone about their name pronunciation if you're not used to doing this. Normalizing this exchange will lead to increased respect and honoring the legacy of each of our families. And we could all use a little more respect in our lives.

I am so proud to be Hitha Nagini Palepu. I've found shortcuts to help others pronounce it properly ("Hitha, like 'hit the ball'") and uncomplainingly spell it when I'm ordering coffee or placing an order over the phone.

I will gently and patiently correct someone if they pronounce my name incorrectly until they've mastered it. I've added a phonetic pronunciation (along with my pronouns) in my email signature.

My name is my power, my history, my wildest dreams, my identity. Your name is all those things as well. It represents your family's history and future, and their hopes and dreams for you. Your name carries great power. Speak your name with pride. Share the meaning and history of your name with others. There will be times when your name will be mispronounced, or callously mocked. Respond with grace, dignity, and a firm look, just as Kamala would. And if you're interrupted, cut it off with a knowing smile and a curt "I'm speaking."

Your name might be the first thing someone learns about you, but it does not define you. You define your name with your experiences, goals, dreams, and values. You may carry the name of your ancestors, but you define your future. You are the product of all these multitudes.

Like all of us, Kamala Harris is a woman of multitudes.

She was the first woman, first Black person, and first South Asian person to be elected attorney general of

California, and before that, all of these firsts to be elected district attorney of San Francisco. She is also a devoted wife, stepmother, sister, aunt, godmother, and friend. Kamala loves to cook and Sunday night dinners are a beloved tradition in her home. She is as strong as she is warm, tough as she is thoughtful, and kind as she is a cunning questioner. How did Kamala cultivate these qualities and become the woman she is today?

THE MATRIARCH OF THE HARRIS FAMILY

Before Kamala grew into these multitudes, she was the firstborn of Shyamala Gopalan Harris, a woman of multitudes herself. Shyamala was a leading cancer researcher, an ardent civil rights activist, and a devoted mother. Shyamala refused to allow anyone to define her by just one thing, and she passed that same wisdom on to her daughters. "Don't let anyone tell you who you are — *you* tell them who you are" was a common lesson repeated to all the Harris women, and it's one that they all live by.

Shyamala's parents — Kamala and Maya's grandparents — P. V. Gopalan and Rajam Gopalan, lived a traditional life by some regards. They were born to Tamil Brahmin families (the upper caste in Hinduism), their marriage arranged by their families. P. V. began his career as a stenographer for the British government, and served in the Indian government after independence. Rajam focused on raising their four children and getting the family settled in their new home every few years, due to P. V.'s job.

When it came to their four children, P. V. and Rajam prioritized education and letting each child forge their own path over arranging marriages with other Tamil Brahmin families. The typical path for a woman like Shyamala was to marry a man selected by her parents, raise a family, and teach singing (she was an accomplished singer in India and won a national competition as a teen). With her family's blessing and financial support, Shyamala immigrated to the United States in 1958 to earn her PhD in nutrition and endocrinology at the University of California, Berkeley.

Shyamala was one of twelve thousand Indians in the United States at the time, as the Luce–Celler Act of 1946 allowed only one hundred Indians into the United States per year. She landed in a rapidly changing America: one that was leading a new global order and had a rising civil rights movement. Berkeley was an epicenter for the protests against the Vietnam War and for civil rights, and Shyamala quickly made herself at home. She found friendship and community in the Afro-American Association, a study group at Cal that discussed the works of Black writers. This group would go on to inspire the formation of the Black Panther Party in 1966, help establish the academic field of African American studies, and help elect Ronald V. Dellums as the mayor of Oakland and to the United States Congress. The group would quickly restrict its membership to people of African descent, with Shyamala being the exception.

She found her family in the Afro-American Association, meeting her future husband at a meeting. Donald Harris was a man of multitudes himself, a scholar seeking a PhD in economics and to break away from the British culture that still lingered in his home country of Jamaica. The scholarship he won from the British colonial government was traditionally redeemed at a university in England, but he chose to head to the west coast of America instead. Gopalan and Harris bonded over their similar paths to California from British-held territories, their shared passion for civil rights, and finding their chosen family in the Afro-American Association.

Shyamala and Donald's marriage ended when Kamala was five, and her friends from the Afro-American Association stepped in to support Shyamala and her two daughters however they could. It was through these friends that Shyamala and the girls met Regina Shelton, whom Kamala refers to as her second mother. Kamala and Maya joined Shelton's children after school, on Sundays at the 23rd Avenue Church of God, and for visits to the family farm in a neighboring town. Kamala and Maya joined the Shelton family on outings to expose them to African American culture, and they participated in the lively discussions that followed. Shyamala's career moved their family to Montreal, where she received tenure at McGill University. Oakland was always home base for the Harris women, and Kamala and Maya returned to the Sheltons' home every summer until they finally moved back to California. Shelton's table was where Kamala would return to for a hug, advice, and Southern home cooking early in her career.

Shyamala gave her all to each of her primary roles — scientist, activist, mother — and defined herself by all of them.

HOW KAMALA OWNS HER MULTITUDES — AND HOW TO DO THE SAME

Kamala's certainty in her multitudes was forged by her mother, and her grandparents before her. Kamala Harris has made history not just for being the first to do many things, but for being many firsts at the same time. In her acceptance speech at the Democratic National Convention, she said Shyamala "raised us to be proud, strong Black women. And she raised us to know and be proud of our Indian heritage." When talking about the family that supported her, she mentioned her *chithi*s and Mrs. Shelton in the same breath. Kamala Harris is proud to be a Black, South Asian woman. She is proudly American.

And yet, her critics and some members of the press portray her otherwise. People have tried to minimize Kamala into narrow tropes to sell a story or win a debate. They look for slivers of her career or identity to paint a superficial portrait of her—someone who is not Black enough, not Indian enough, too mean during a Senate hearing, laughs too much in a debate. Nearly every woman can empathize with their multitudes being hacked away and their whole self reduced to a caricature.

Kamala's strength was forged in being "the first" so many times in her career, with the weight of expectations and the higher bar that is set for women, and especially women of color. Your experiences can weigh you down, but they can also fuel your fire. Kamala has been insulted, mocked, and her record misrepresented to millions of Americans over the course of her career. But she forges on, with relentless preparation and total certainty in herself. She knows how to filter constructive criticism from childish taunts and shallow insults, and the latter says more about those who speak them than it will ever say about her.

How will you show up, with the full power of your name and your multitudes? You need confidence, and you need to be ready to guide.

Confidence is tricky. It's become synonymous with affirmations, pleas to "love yourself," and an effective marketing tool to sell everything from T-shirts to personal care products. But there is no substitute for pure belief in yourself. When wielded fully, it becomes your armor and shields you from the negativity that comes your way.

While cultivating confidence is a lifelong journey, the idea of "borrowed confidence" can help accelerate it. Coined by leadership expert Darrah Brustein, it's borrowing the confidence others have in you until you begin to believe and own it for yourself. Create a hype file—a place to save screenshots of emails, DMs, and texts, and voice messages or videos showcasing the wonderful things people tell you about yourself. Whenever you need a boost, review the file and go on to win the challenge ahead of you.

My hype file is an album in my photos app. I go back and reread the emails from mentors and old partners when I get a rejection from a potential investor or partner. When I second-guess whether to share a specific topic or my personal thoughts on a sensitive issue in #5SmartReads, I go back and reread an email from someone who told me that #5SmartReads helped her hold her own in a political conversation with her father. If I've had a hard day wrangling my boys, I watch the videos of them hugging and playing nicely, or the recordings of Rho telling me, "Mommy, I love you. You're the best mommy!" Don't restrict your hype file to your career or school. You are a woman of multitudes, and your hype file should represent your best in all of your multidimensional glory.

Confidence is only one part of owning your multitudes. The other is guiding how others perceive you. Kamala is a master guide, and uses every public opportunity to her advantage. When you watch her in a

Senate Judiciary hearing, you can't help but be impressed (and a little intimidated) with her rapid questions, attention to detail, and composure. In both her DNC and VP acceptance speeches, you feel deeply connected to her as she recounts her childhood and the women who inspired and raised her. And as she teaches Senator Mark Warner to make a tuna fish sandwich over Instagram, you can't help but laugh and crave one of those sandwiches yourself. In every moment, Harris is guiding us to feel and see her fully, but also to focus on specific aspects of her personality and background she wants to highlight.

Guiding is the third step outlined in EDGE, a leadership framework created by Harvard Business School professor Laura Huang. She defines it as a way to "reframe potentially negative perceptions," and it starts with putting yourself in someone else's shoes to understand how they see you. Does that vision differ from the value you bring to the table, and if so, how can you bridge that divide? You can take a page from Harris's book by using your words carefully, and showing the work. Harris always speaks the truth and is careful in the words she chooses, knowing full well that how something is defined will influence how we think about it. Delivery and performance have been trumped over the truth in recent years, but there is power in a clear message rooted in the facts. Show the work that helped you arrive at this position: the steps taken, the information used, the other options considered. Harris calls this technique "showing the math," and it's how she has prepared her closing arguments, evaluated policies and proposals, and taught others to do the same.

Guiding is easier said than done. Questions are the key to successful guiding—the more open-ended, the better. When I pitch to a potential investor, I ask them to share a previous successful investment, and the specific factors that made the investment successful. I ask how they support their portfolio companies between raises, or how they've assisted in any exit transactions. If I'm meeting with a potential sponsor, I ask them what the goals are for the campaign. Is it downloads of an app, purchases, or general awareness? I ask what metrics matter the most to them, and why. I request best practices and examples of previous successful engagements. Getting the answers to these questions helps you understand exactly how you may be viewed negatively, and it allows you to proactively address those concerns.

For example, if an investor had concerns about how small our team was, I would respond with a story of how our founder (and my father) helped develop the formulation of Veletri (an enhanced formulation of epoprostenol, which treats pulmonary arterial hypertension). The product was developed in his first lab, a two-room apartment above a horse stable in Hyderabad, with the same core people that continue to work for him seventeen years later. The story would flow into how this team successfully did the same for other thriving pharmaceutical products. I'd end the story with our development expenses sheet, demonstrating that a lean, highly productive team allows for the funds to be focused on development and commercialization—not extraneous overhead or unnecessary expenses.

There is no substitute for hard work and knowing your facts inside out, which we will tackle in the next chapter. But asking thoughtful questions to understand the person's concerns or beliefs and telling a story that addresses them pointedly is a skill worth cultivating and practicing. It creates a clear line between the person you are and the work you're doing, helping to establish healthy boundaries to protect your energy and your multitudes.

There will be instances where confidence and guiding won't sway others' opinions of you. Knowing exactly who you are and what you stand for gives you the strength to bring your whole self to the world, and shrug off those who try to minimize it. Kamala Devi Harris brings her whole self and tells the world exactly who she is at every moment. She's the daughter of Shyamala Gopalan Harris, and sister to Maya Harris. She's a proud Black and South Asian woman. She's been the first woman and person of color to be elected district attorney of San Francisco and attorney general of California. She was California's first Black senator, and the first South Asian to be elected to the Senate. As vice president, she is many firsts: the first woman, first Black VP, first VP of South Asian descent. She is all of these multitudes, and more. And no one is going to tell the world who Kamala Harris is — only SHE will.

CONNECTING THE DOTS OF YOUR MULTITUDES

by Esther Ayorinde

I am a woman of multitudes.

I've spent the past fifteen years at a Fortune 100 technology company, starting in sales in various industries like entertainment, media, and sports, and working my way up to a global executive role. I'm an active mentor and public speaker. I've also danced professionally in the NFL and the NBA for seven seasons, five of these while at the technology company. This professional dance career earned me the title as the first Black captain (group leader) on the Jets Flight Crew as well as a feature in the San Francisco 49ers Museum. I've enjoyed being a choreographer, teaching dance with various dance studios and professional teams. I'm most proud of my advocacy for young girls in STEM and the arts, both as a board member for a nonprofit in Silicon Valley as well as growing a dance and self-esteem camps company that empowered hundreds of young girls through our programs across the US.

Hitha calls this being a multihyphenate. I call it intentional congruence.

While I may have found myself in tech, dance, and entrepreneurship in seemingly random ways, each of these passions has influenced and amplified the others throughout my career. They've helped me identify and accept new opportunities, work smarter, and be unapologetically myself. I can't do all these things without them feeding one another in some way.

Intentional congruence is the principle of each aspect of something feeding the other. This is a practice that helps me stay the course in pursuing my multifaceted passions while striving for success.

Think about Whom This Serves. There are plenty of things I can do. What I choose to do has to tie back in to how this will help make an impact in the world. From high school to my early years at Cisco, I continued to work as a dance teacher and cocktail waitress or bartender to help support my family and my goals. Later in my career, I was offered the opportunity to help build Cisco's growth strategy for Africa. The job gave me an opportunity to connect to the place my parents fled forty years ago as well as leverage the power of a Fortune 100 company to contribute to the continent that will have the largest working-age population in the next ten to fifteen years. Whether serving a steak or transforming go-to-market opportunities in emerging countries, each of these opportunities served me personally and professionally, and prepared me for future opportunities that I didn't realize were possible.

Prioritize Ruthlessly. One of my mentors taught me how to reclaim my thinking time. Every Sunday, she looks over her calendar and cuts out about 40 percent of what's there that doesn't move her closer to her priorities, and creates more space to think. Take a step back, look at the big picture, and do some planning. The amount of time you waste in the spin of reactive work is a lot, and investing this time makes you and your team more productive. I've seen the impact of this practice myself, and it's one I try to do as often as I can. If you're just starting out, filter every item on your calendar and the emails awaiting a response and ask yourself, "Is this the best and most effective use of my time?" Doing this will help you understand where you should be spending your time for maximum impact *or* maximum satisfaction.

Make Time to Play. I couldn't rely on dancing as my sole form of work — I needed something stable and consistent, and that brought in a solid income. I made the time to continue dancing in the NFL and NBA while studying at college and in my early years at Cisco because I needed that space to be unapologetically feminine. Dance gave me that outlet and allowed me to stay connected in the community, but also gave me the time to build my career and to make the switch into the more masculine world of technology easier. Dancing in the NFL and NBA also taught me a lot of skills — both as a businesswoman and about sports in general — that has helped me advance my career, from talking about last night's game with a client to helping brainstorm the sports solutions at my company.

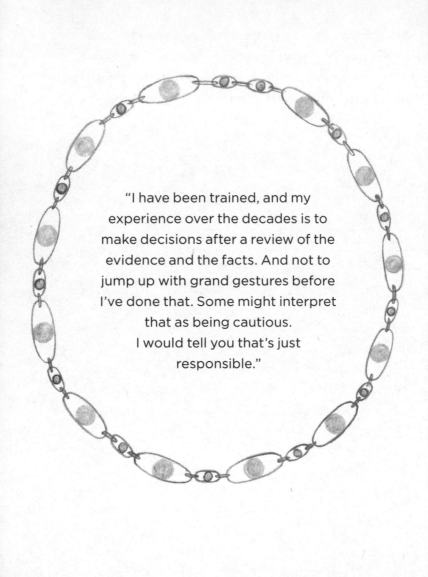

"I have been trained, and my experience over the decades is to make decisions after a review of the evidence and the facts. And not to jump up with grand gestures before I've done that. Some might interpret that as being cautious.
I would tell you that's just responsible."

CHAPTER 2

"Do Something About It—And Don't Do It Half-Assed"

Shyamala Gopalan Harris did not tolerate idle words or idle hands. As they were growing up, when Kamala and her sister, Maya, weren't in school, they were in constant motion. They helped their mom in the lab on weekends, cleaning test tubes and pipettes. They sang in their church choir every Sunday and took piano and ballet lessons. If the TV was on, their hands would be busy working on needlepoint or crocheting. Shyamala was focused on keeping the girls busy, and always doing things. "Doing something" spilled into other areas of their lives as well. If the girls came home upset about something that happened in school, their mother responded, "Well, what did you do?"

One of the truths Kamala held as a child was

knowing the world was an unjust place. She joined her parents at demonstrations and peaceful protests as a toddler. Mrs. Shelton's day care was decorated with posters of Black leaders in history, their stories told to Kamala and the other children who spent their after-school hours there. She also bore witness to how organizing and communities could drive change. On Thursday evenings, Shyamala and the girls would head to the Rainbow Sign, an Oakland community center that was founded by eleven Black women who had been pioneers in their respective fields: journalism, medicine, and television. Families with young children were welcome, the food was plentiful, and the energy was electric. As a young child, Harris saw Nina Simone perform, heard Shirley Chisholm speak as she explored her presidential run, and listened to readings from Maya Angelou and Alice Walker. James Baldwin was a regular guest.

Shyamala taught the girls to "fight systems in a way that causes them to be fairer, and don't be limited by what has always been." Harris saw these words come to life at the Rainbow Sign, especially in the meetings of Black Women Organized for Political Action. BWOPA's mission was "to bring to bear on politics the strong power that Black women have exercised in religion and education," and they focused their efforts in electing more Black men and women to office. The chapter at the Rainbow Sign helped elect Representative Ron Dellums and Berkeley mayor Warren Widener to their offices. Widener later returned to the center to interview Nina Simone and declare March 31, 1972, as Nina Simone Day.

The girls took these words to heart at a young age. When Kamala was ten and Maya was eight, they rallied their neighbors to build a playground in the empty courtyard of their apartment building. They mounted a similar campaign in Montreal, leading a successful demonstration in front of their building to be able to play soccer on the lawn. Harris was even successful at lobbying her mother in changing schools, from their neighborhood school for native French speakers to a fine arts middle school.

Their mother's response slightly changed as Kamala and Maya entered high school. If they appeared to be getting distracted, their mother would say, "Don't do anything half-assed." At Westmount High in Montreal, Kamala was working on the yearbook and singing with the Pep Club at school events, in addition to excelling in her studies. With her best friend Wanda Kagan and four other girls, she danced in a troupe at school and for elderly members of the community. But when Wanda confided that her stepfather was molesting her, Kamala jumped into action and moved her friend into her home. Wanda shared a room with Kamala and fondly remembers the warmth of the Harris home—Indian food simmering on the stove, mandatory studying after school, and helping with chores. The months Wanda lived with the Harris family made an impact on her life. "They planted the seed of stability and empowerment in me," said Kagan, who named her daughter Maya and now works at Jewish General Hospital (where Shyamala had worked in the Lady Davis Institute). She and Kamala are still close friends.

Kagan's experience stirred something in Kamala. It was one of many examples of her heeding her mother's words to "do something about it," but this was more than organizing neighborhood kids for the right to play or bringing her dance troupe to entertain elderly people in Montreal. She was able to help her friend, but how many other children were facing the same situation and could not seek help? She knew the world was an unjust place. How could she help make it more just? There isn't a single moment that led to Kamala's desire to become a lawyer, but the seeds were planted throughout her life. She listened to the conversations her grandfather and his friends had on the role of government and fighting corruption as they walked on the beach in Chennai. In Oakland, she saw how family friend Sherman L. Williams was sought out when someone was in need. In becoming a lawyer, she could help individuals seek justice under the law. But in helping Wanda, she saw that the system itself needed reform. She recounted Wanda's experience in a campaign video, crediting it with her desire to become a prosecutor so she could protect people like her.

She pursued her goal through her undergraduate work at Howard University and law school at Hastings, a public law school in San Francisco affiliated with the University of California system, and as a clerk in Alameda County's district attorney's office. An example of the path Kamala wanted to forge as a prosecutor who would be true to her values happened early on when she was assisting a case in Alameda that involved a drug bust. An innocent bystander—a woman with young children at home—had been jailed along with those charged. With most of the office already gone for the weekend, Kamala rushed to the clerk of the court on a Friday afternoon to have the case called immediately, so the woman could return to her family instead of spending the weekend in jail. The judge gave the order to free the woman. While this case is one that rarely is mentioned in Kamala's record, it's one of the most significant for her. "It was revelatory, a moment that proved how much it mattered to have compassionate people working as prosecutors," Kamala wrote in her memoir. That case solidified her goal to not just become a prosecutor, but reimagine the role from what it had previously been.

After passing the bar, Kamala did just that. She spent nine years as an assistant district attorney of Alameda County, the latter part prosecuting sex crimes. Prosecuting rapists and child molesters is not for the faint of heart, but it's core to the vision of a compassionate prosecutor that Kamala had imagined for herself. Much of her time was spent at Highland General Hospital in Oakland, where she met with survivors. Kamala prepared some victims to testify in court, and was simply there to listen to others. She spent time hearing their stories, walking them through what testifying would be like, and giving them a safe space to process their trauma. When the survivors were young children, she had the daunting task of evaluating if they were capable of testifying, as well as willing. Kamala played for hours with a six-year-old girl who was being molested by her sixteen-year-old brother, trying to build trust and see if the young girl could explain what had happened. In the end, the little girl was unable to testify and Kamala didn't have enough evidence to charge her brother. The experience left her in tears and feeling completely powerless.

As Shyamala had impressed upon her and Maya, it also inspired her to do more. Kamala leapt at the opportunity to move to the San Francisco city attorney's office to oversee the child and family services division, with a promise that she could focus on policy as well as cases. Her first initiative was establishing a task force to study the issues of sexually exploited youth, and she partnered with Norma Hotaling to lead the effort. Norma had lived these issues firsthand and had created SAGE (Standing Against Global Exploitation), which offered trauma-informed care in rehabilitating former sex workers and helped them heal and transition out of the trade. Together, Norma and Kamala saw that there were no safe places for youth involved in sex work to access. Kamala knew that many of them had run away from foster care or didn't have parents in the picture. Often, their pimps and older sex workers were all they had in terms of security and care. Sex workers were disproportionately arrested (instead of their pimps), and would return to their pimps after being released by the police. The task force proposed a number of measures within their power to address this problem. A safe house with resources to keep these young people secure, healthy, and able to return to school was one of the proposals, along with a public education campaign to get the word out. Posters were hung in buses and public bathrooms, where at-risk youth would be able to get the details. The task force also proposed that law enforcement fully investigate the brothels hiding in plain sight as massage parlors and take action. While reforming the foster care system would be the best solution for eliminating the pipeline of sex workers, it was well beyond Kamala's powers at the city attorney's office. The proposal was approved and funded by San Francisco's board of supervisors, with dozens of minors rescued and more than thirty brothels shut down in the first couple of years. The task force formalized a warm relationship between the city and SAGE, which worked collaboratively to help girls and women safely transition from sex work until Norma's passing in 2008.

"All those times my mother had pressed me—'Well, what did *you* do?'—suddenly made a lot more sense," Kamala wrote. "I realized I didn't have to wait for someone else to take the lead; I could start making things happen on my own."

Doing something about the issues you care about—and not doing it half-assed—sounds simple enough. Actually carrying it through is quite another thing, and can be daunting and seemingly impossible. You know the tried-and-true advice: break down the task into smaller pieces, put your phone away while you work, limit distractions, and so on. But how do you actually start, and then keep going?

Let's start with starting. I am a master avoider of starting my own big work. I would rather check my social media accounts one last time or scan through my emails and tackle any urgent responses before getting down to the task at hand. I get overwhelmed by the scale of some of my projects (this book included!), and I let that anxiety take over my actions. Over time, I've discovered my "start triggers," the rituals, behaviors, and micro-actions I can take to nudge my brain out of emotion and into action. Rather than focusing on the actual task at hand, I focus on my list of start triggers and give them my full attention. As I was writing this book, the list looked like this:

- put my phone in a drawer
- close out all email, social media, and messaging apps

- open my writing app and my research spreadsheet
- turn on my writing playlist
- take a deep breath, pull my shoulders down, and jut my chin out
- write one sentence. And then another. One more.

I've also developed different start triggers for different tasks. I have one for tackling email, another for updating financial models and pitch decks, one for reviewing documents and presentations from others, and even one for just putting down my phone when I'm sucked into a black hole of scrolling. Micro-actions are incredibly important in helping us pause, reassess, and refocus. Starting on starting has transformed how I work and live. Starting is great, but it's also not enough to get you across the finish line.

In any project you take on—small or large—you will face setbacks, rejections, overhauls, and people who are difficult to work with. The work that will make the biggest impact will have all of these, most of the time. You have to fill up your own cup to bring your best self to the task (which we'll tackle in Chapter 4), and you need to check in with yourself regularly throughout the project. I have tried a number of tools and frameworks for my own check-ins, but none have been as successful as following the three questions Stacey Abrams asks herself:

1. What do I want?
2. Why do I want it?
3. How do I get it?

"Figure out what the 'why' is for you, because jumping from the 'what' to the 'do' is meaningless if you don't know why," Abrams said in her TED Talk. "Because when it gets hard, when it gets tough, when your friends walk away from you, when your supporters forget you, when you don't win your first race—if you don't know why, you can't try again."

I come back to these questions when I'm feeling low in any project or task. I also find myself returning to the three pieces of advice Abrams gave when she delivered the keynote speech at the Riveter Summit:

1. Don't edit your ambition.
2. Don't go it alone.
3. Don't forget the pain.

In order to successfully get things done—small or large—you need to keep the end goal in mind. For

Kamala, it was to lower the number of youth entering the criminal justice system. For Abrams, recently, it was to deliver Georgia to Joe Biden and Kamala Harris in the 2020 presidential election *and* send Reverend Raphael Warnock and Jon Ossoff to the Senate. It's very easy to celebrate the successes, but we often gloss over the hard work, the challenges, the mistakes, and the opposition that both faced in pursuit of their goals. Issues will come up. You will face setbacks. The worst-case scenario will be the reality you face. Whenever that happens, come back to your why. Visualize the future that you are building. Reach out to the people in the fight with you, and create space for everyone to share their feelings and ideas. Edit the plan, and get back to work. And if the work is overwhelming, start on starting.

This may sound obvious, but you will also have to put in the work. A tireless work ethic is the worst-kept secret behind every successful person. For Black women—who have to work twice as hard to get half as far—a strong work ethic isn't an option. It's a necessity. For Kamala, it was modeled by her mother. "She had only two goals in life: to raise her two daughters and to end breast cancer," Kamala wrote in her memoir. "She pushed us hard and with high expectations as she nurtured us. And all the while, she made Maya and me feel special, like we could do anything we wanted to if we put in the work."

Kamala's work ethic did not go unnoticed. "She was energetic, willing to take tough cases, laser focused, driven to be successful. She knew early where to get the education she needed. She paid very close attention when old-timers were talking," remarked Nancy O'Malley, Alameda County district attorney.

There is no secret to hard work. It requires clarity on what needs to get done and a plan to get it done. Author Laura Vanderkam has written multiple books and delivered a TED Talk on productivity, and she encourages us to check our emotions at the door of our work. "We can get caught up in how we feel about things. But that doesn't always matter in the pursuit of a larger goal," she told me. "Say you need to call these five people out of the blue in order to make something happen. There are steps you can take—maybe get a warm introduction to them—but eventually you'll have to pick up the phone and just do it. Tell yourself 'I don't have to enjoy it' or 'I don't have to feel good about it, but eventually I will be on the other side of it.' And eventually, you'll be happy to say, 'I have done it.'" Instead of focusing on how you feel right now, focus on your future self.

Kamala had her eyes set on higher office early on in her career, and worked tirelessly to make that goal a reality. What is your big goal? What vision do you have for your future self? When you find yourself making excuses to procrastinate, check in with that future self and think about them in detail. How are you spending your days? Where are you living? What are you doing, and what impact are you making? Focus on the details that bring you joy and inspiration. And then get to it. Send the email. Schedule the meeting. Begin your research. If you want to live your future self's life, you have to work for it.

It's also important to examine your time and identify the things you're doing because you think you should, not because you want to. Center your schedule on the things you want and only you can do: work, sleep, take care of yourself, spend time with your family, take up hobbies that bring you joy. Check in with yourself on the things you think you should do, and examine if there's something that you can offload to a roommate or partner or let go entirely. It is okay if the toys aren't picked up or there are piles of paper on your desk or the dishes have piled up in the sink one night. We build expectations of what life should look like, but we have the choice to make our rules. You get to make these choices based on what works for your life. For me, it means my clean laundry sits in my basket until it's time to wash another load. My desk is buried under piles of books and papers and snacks, but I wrote this book and ran my company from this cluttered mess. That said, waking up to a sink full of dishes stresses me out, so my husband and I trade off on doing the dishes every evening and constantly remind our kids to put theirs directly in the dishwasher.

"Once a second is gone, no amount of money in the world can buy you that second back," Vanderkam says. Privilege, money, and different phases of life will always be there, but we all have the same twenty-four hours every single day. How can you spend more of those hours doing the things you want to do, rather than the things you feel obligated to do? The answer is doing the hard things, and letting go of others. Only you know what those things are for you. In the wise words of Shyamala, "Focus on what's in front of you and the rest will follow."

THE RIGHT THINGS ARE THE HARDEST THINGS

Kamala's work ethic was tested when she was elected district attorney of San Francisco. Dressed in a Donald Deal suit she'd purchased for the occasion, she was sworn in on the same day as Gavin Newsom (the new mayor of San Francisco), signaling a changing of the guard in the city's leadership. After being sworn in, she immediately walked to her new office. It was an empty room, save for a metal cabinet with a Wang computer from the 1980s balanced on it and a chair. No desk. Kamala took a seat, took out a yellow notepad from her briefcase, and got to work. She began jotting down a to-do list, organized by short term (a couple of weeks), medium term (a couple of years), and long term (as long as it takes).

Kamala tackled the short-term tasks quickly, like ordering new computers and copiers and literally cleaning up the office for her team. Restoring the culture of the district attorney's office, which had languished under her predecessor Terence Hallinan, was a medium-term goal. Kamala established weekly meetings with the felony trial lawyers in the office for them to present their cases and verdicts to their colleagues. She created space for each lawyer to share and receive feedback on the details of the case, like how the defense presented, the judge's response, how the witnesses fared, the verdict. No matter the verdict, Kamala led the applause after each lawyer's report to celebrate their individual work. These meetings defined the culture of the district attorney's office under Kamala. She held her team to exacting standards—in how they prepared for cases, in taking pride in their appearance and dressing professionally, and in having a deep understanding of the community they served. "I'd tell my team to learn about the communities where they didn't live, to follow neighborhood news, to go to local festivals and community forums. 'For the people' means for *them*. All of them."

Once the culture of the district attorney's office was back in place, Kamala focused on the long-term goals on the list. As a prosecutor, Kamala made a difference case by case. Leading a division, she created policies that helped dozens of people. As district attorney, she could impact the lives of hundreds of the most vulnerable San Franciscans, and really do something about the problems she had witnessed firsthand.

"I want to speak to Kamala. I will only speak to Kamala." Women marched into the district attorney's office speaking these words. Kamala would meet them in the lobby and walk them back into her office, where they would burst into tears and fall into her arms. These were often the mothers who had tragically lost their children to gun violence. More than seventy homicide cases were unsolved when Kamala was sworn in as district attorney, and these mothers continued to grieve.

"He still matters to me," one told Kamala. "He matters to me, too," she replied. Reducing the number of homicides and sparing the lives of young Black men was a long-term goal, but Kamala took decisive action in the near term. She called in a squad of homicide detectives to her office, asking for details about every unsolved case and pressing them on different approaches to solve them. The detectives didn't expect Kamala's rapid-fire questions and pressure, and the meeting was far different than any they had had with Hallinan. But it resulted in a new campaign from the police department encouraging witnesses to step forward. In time, 25 percent of the unsolved homicide cases were closed and justice was served.

Resolving homicide cases brought closure to existing problems, but did nothing to address the root cause.

In her first visit to the county jail, Kamala saw the people behind the crimes. Many suffered from addiction and were the victims of structural poverty. Some were fathers. Some were young adults who had joined gangs as a means to survive, with no other options available to them. Most of them were jailed for nonviolent offenses, and had little hope to return to civil society. This visit stuck with Kamala during her years as a prosecutor. As district attorney, she could do something about it.

Kamala convened a small group she trusted wholeheartedly. She asked a single question: "What would it take to put together a reentry program that actually worked?" In the early 2000s, justice across the country was quite punitive. The job of a prosecutor was to put people in prison, not help them be released. Reentry was not a priority for justice departments nor legislatures. Despite the hostile environment and backlash from her colleagues, Kamala pushed back. Her upbringing was rooted in doing what was right, and she chose to become a prosecutor to change how justice was delivered. Offering those who had paid their debt to society a way to reenter it successfully was just and right. And as district attorney, she had an opportunity to do just that.

Back on Track was born. The program was rigorous

by design, combining therapy with drug testing, volunteer hours with GED courses and job training, and classes focused on parenting and financial literacy. Only nonviolent first-time offenders were eligible for this yearlong program. In order to participate, each member had to earn their GED and secure a job, remain drug-free the entire time, and pay all outstanding child support if applicable over the course of the program. Each participant had to plead guilty, and successful completion and graduation from it would also result in having their charges expunged. The district attorney's office ran the program, but it was a community-wide effort. Local trade unions offered apprenticeship opportunities, and Goodwill Industries led the employment training and volunteering. The San Francisco Chamber of Commerce and its member companies helped Back on Track participants find jobs.

Not only did Back on Track help the participants, but it also offered a significant return on investment for San Francisco. The program cost $50,000 per participant, whereas it cost the city just as much to prosecute a felony case and house someone in county jail for a year. In the first two years of the program, only 10 percent of the graduates had reoffended (compared to the usual 50 percent reoffender rate for similar crimes). In time,

Back on Track became a model for other justice departments. The Justice Department under President Obama adopted Back on Track at the federal level. What was deeply unpopular nearly twenty years ago is now a model for civil society.

Kamala and her team deserve the credit for Back on Track's success, but the program's success partners also share in that credit. Declaring your support and claiming yourself an ally is not enough to solve the problems in our communities and in our workplaces. Goodwill Industries, the trade unions, and the Chamber of Commerce didn't just allow their name and logo to be used for Back on Track. They invested their resources, time, and capital to actively participate in the program, and they share in the program's success. Allyship is cheap. Investment is how real change happens.

"Doing something about it" doesn't always mean what you personally do. It's also about how you show up for others in your work, particularly the women of color, who are largely underpaid, undervalued, and overlooked. Allyship is largely passive, defined by what we say or write. Being a success partner means you're using your power to create opportunities for others, as Minda Harts, the CEO of The Memo, a career development platform for women of color, explores in her book of the same name. "Get to know the women of color in your office. When promotions come up, consider them! Half the battle is that you aren't even thinking about retaining and advancing us. It all goes back to a mindset: you don't consider many of us leaders because you've never seen us lead, but we rarely get the opportunity to advance into leadership roles that would demonstrate our ability to lead. Do you see how this is a recurring theme taking place across industries? If you are tired of us talking about it, be part of the solution to fix it! Being inclusive is not some hard code to crack; the remedy is simple—be intentional!"

If you are in a position of power, it really is as simple as this. Study the meetings that fill up your calendar. How many of those are mentorship and networking meetings? Who are the people you're meeting with? Are they a diverse group of people from all areas of the company, or are they all the same gender and race? Take some time to attend various employee resource group meetings and connect with some new people in the company. Let them know you're eager to get to know them, and accept the meetings and continue the conversation when they reach out.

If there's an opening on your team, make sure the

job is being posted to new job boards and networks that are built by and for communities that you are invested in hiring from. Things won't change unless you do, and the actions you can take are straightforward and simple. You just have to do it.

If you're looking for your success partner, keep reading. The next chapter is how to play the political game that exists in every workplace and school. Not playing is not an option, and you will need to play to win to make your goals a reality.

Build diverse relationships. Outwork everyone. Stay focused on the vision of your future self. Start on starting. You have big goals and dreams. Do something about them. And don't do it half-assed.

HOW I DID SOMETHING ABOUT IT

by Mandana Dayani

A few months after the birth of our second daughter, Miller, I saw a breaking news headline across my television with flashing images of migrant children separated from their families, under aluminum blankets and in cages. I felt all my insides start to implode. What happened to the country that welcomed me and my family as refugees just thirty years earlier? How did we become so divided?

I booked a trip to Tornillo, Texas. I had to see the camps.

I don't think I had any idea how profoundly that trip would impact the rest of my life. As I walked up to the fences that separated me from the camps, I knew instantly that I needed to do something to help bring our country back together.

The next few months were spent learning, questioning, dreaming, challenging, in meeting after meeting, until it became clear: The path to effecting the most significant change would be through increased voter participation. I knew exactly the incredible women it would take to make it happen.

Over the last three years, I have had the unimaginable privilege of working every day with these women, who are both my friends and mentors, who came together to build **I am a voter.** into the incredible organization it is today. Together, we have helped change the culture around civic engagement, making it more mainstream, cool, and integral to one's personal identity. We dreamt a new vision for how we show up for our country and one another. We did it not only by completely reimagining how we approach this topic, but by knowing that we could never do it on our own.

The story of **I am a voter.**'s success is one that is owned by so many. It was a movement created by people, volunteers, brands, companies, and everything in between, and it was only possible because we empowered anyone who wanted to participate to leverage all their personal and professional relationships and to contribute whatever they could (e.g., branded store windows, free ad space, merchandise, content, social media, etc.), no matter how big or small. It became the perfect intersection of passion, hustle, and hope. Every day, every person on this team showed up with their whole heart and left everything on the field. We know we have so much more work to do, but by charting our own path and challenging the status quo, we will continue to make a difference.

Here are a few things I learned that I would love to pass on:

- **Find your people.** Surround yourself with people who inspire you, who make you feel anything is possible, who validate your dreams and make you want to be bigger and better.

- **Listen to that nagging voice you hear as you put your head on your pillow at night.** You know that thing you know you want to do, but aren't sure you can? Do it. You can.

- **Don't wait until you know everything before you start anything.** You will never know everything. You will never be fully prepared. None of us are. Learning is part of the journey.

- **Never lose your curiosity.** It will guide your creativity to forge new paths.

- **Anger is a very useful tool.** Use it to drive you and to remind you why your work is important.

- **Know that we are stronger together.** The exclusive, you-can't-sit-with-us BS mentality has never worked. Always leave seats at the table for those who want to pitch in.

- **Fail fast.** If something isn't working — whether it be a personal relationship, campaign idea, or job — pivot. Move on. Find a better way.

- **Think bigger.** Challenge yourself to change the system, even if it is in incremental ways. Incremental change starts the snowball effect to large, earth-shifting change. Envision the goal and charge forward.

- **Build community.** Have I said this enough? Our collective well-being will always be dependent on the health, safety, and prosperity of one another. Fight for justice for all.

Lastly, to anyone who tells you to stay in your lane, make sure to tell them to *&%$ off.

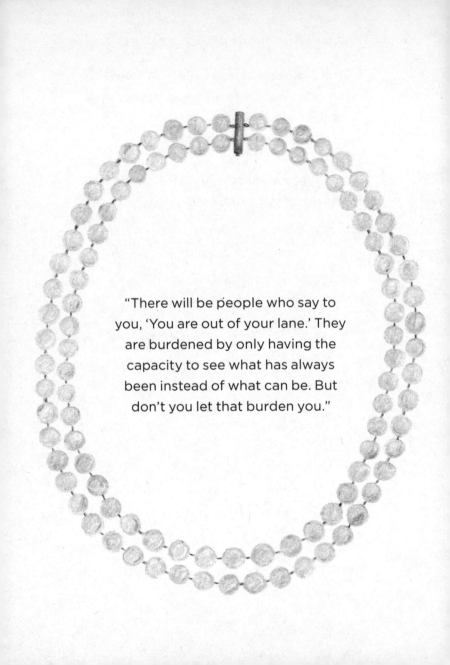

"There will be people who say to you, 'You are out of your lane.' They are burdened by only having the capacity to see what has always been instead of what can be. But don't you let that burden you."

CHAPTER 3

Acting on Your Ambition

When Kamala Harris was ready to run for district attorney of San Francisco, she called Andrea Dew Steele. Kamala had met the successful organizer while serving on the boards of WomenCount and Emerge California, both of which Steele had helped create. Not only was Kamala active on the nonprofit scene, but she also befriended members of San Francisco's social elite while serving as a trustee of San Francisco's Museum of Modern Art and attending charity events in the city. These friends would form her finance committee, chaired by Mark Buell. He had met Kamala through his stepdaughter Summer Tompkins Walker, but had originally dismissed her as a socialite with a law degree. Over burgers, she not only convinced him to support her, but he volunteered to lead the committee. Buell's support and Kamala's network helped her earn more than $100,000 for her campaign by the first reporting period.

Kamala continued to bridge her two worlds aptly during the campaign. Her headquarters were in the Bayview district, a predominantly Black neighborhood that had fallen on hard times. Harris arrived at campaign headquarters before sunrise. She campaigned relentlessly at bus stops and outside of grocery stores, her posters duct-taped to an ironing board that held her campaign literature. Over time, the campaign received donations from every ZIP code in the city. While her campaign benefited tremendously from the wealthy donors in the Financial District and Pacific Heights, she earned support throughout San Francisco and won the district attorney's race decisively in the runoff.

Kamala's first campaign was rooted in offering value to every person she came into contact with. With donors, she was a breath of fresh air and a significant change from how the district attorney's office had been run for decades prior. She never took her relationships for granted, and worked for every donation she received. She sought voters throughout the city, fully knowing that they needed to meet her and learn more about her before considering voting for her. Every vote and voter mattered to Kamala.

IT'S ALL ABOUT THE HUSTLE

Offering value is something you can do in any interaction, whether you're reaching out to someone you admire or offering your experiences and advice to someone who's asked you for help. "When we reach out to people for networking, it's very one-sided," said Minda Harts, author of *The Memo*. "If you have value to offer, shoot your shot and do so respectfully and meaningfully." Harts recalled a friend who had noticed a CEO of a Fortune 500 company posting about wanting to be a better leader on social media. Her friend, a career coach who is also a Black woman, looked up his email and wrote him. She introduced herself and the work she'd done, and offered some ways she could help this leader and proposed a meeting. The CEO took her up on it.

If you're a woman just starting your career—especially a woman of color—the game has different rules for you, and they've changed drastically due to COVID-19. The rapid adoption of videoconferencing and remote work gives you a unique opportunity to be visible in a way you haven't been before. If your boss's boss is joining a meeting and you want to build a relationship, show up with the camera on. Participate in the chat and share your ideas on the call. "It's hard for people to be your success partner if no one knows anything about you," Harts told me.

So how exactly do you do that? It's something Esther Ayorinde excels in. Esther and I met in the Sales Associates Program at Cisco. It was an extremely competitive training program, and Esther was consistently one of the top performers as well as one of the kindest and most generous peers in the program. In addition to the demanding program, Esther also worked as a dance instructor and a cocktail waitress to help support her sisters in college and her mother. She coordinated study groups with her team to stay on top of the material (and in leading them, she was able to schedule them around her other two jobs). The groups offered accountability and support in learning the various tech stacks, but they also fostered deep friendships among the group. Esther also took the time to write holiday cards—with personal messages in each one—to every member of the program: associates, managers, and instructors. "Our program was filled with high achievers who would go on to do amazing things," she told me. "I wanted to build the relationship, and this was a way to be remembered ten years from now." Esther is still with

Cisco, having risen the ranks to become the senior director of managed services.

Esther's reasons for building relationships and investing in her career goes beyond her personal career goals. "Coming from African immigrant parents, there was no other place for me to go than up. When you know there will not be privileges afforded to you but you know your worth, it helps you fight for every opportunity and bring value to everything you do," she said. "I didn't have an option to be mediocre, because it was more than just about me. It was helping put my sisters through college and helping my mom, so I absolutely had to make it." Show up, speak up, and follow up. Again, and again, and again. The advice itself is simple, but the effort it requires is more than most are willing to do. Put in the effort, every day.

How good you are at your job will not solely determine your future. It is but one factor of many, and it might be a reason used to keep you in your current position. You have to invest time and energy in understanding the politics of where you work and attend school, and learn how to play the game. To be clear, most of the rules of office politics are based in bias. Bias influences how we show up at work, including how you dress and wear your hair and the names you use (especially if it's a non-anglicized name). It's beyond frustrating to consider how these seemingly meaningless choices will factor in bias among your coworkers and supervisors, but it is a part of our reality today.

My fervent wish is that you own the power of your name and multitudes and show up in your most authentic self with the work ethic to match. But I also caution you to take a second to do a bias check. If your natural hair and beautiful name might raise some eyebrows, prepare your defusing remarks. Prepare the quick story that shares the meaning of your name, and a primer on how to pronounce it. Are your brightly colored outfits attracting attention? Offer a smile and say, "Red is such a powerful color, no? Wearing it gives me some extra energy and helps me work better." If you wear your hair in its natural texture glory, wear it well and proudly. That this burden falls on women — especially women of color — is unfair and frustrating, but it exists and it must be managed. By being proactive, you can claim some control over the situation versus letting yourself be managed by it. Own your narrative and your power, and wield it to your advantage. Sometimes the most powerful qualities are the quiet, unassuming ones.

Stacey Abrams is a master class in showing up in her full power. "I am a sturdy Black woman with natural hair," Abrams told NBC News. "When you close your eyes and imagine the person you think of as a leader, I'm likely not the image that pops into your head." Abrams refused to accept the alterations that advisers recommended when she was running for governor of Georgia. She did, however, consider the list and looked for areas for compromise. "I found a style that met the public imagination of what a leader looks like, but also met my need for comfort and my personality," she told Bustle. "I wear my hair natural, but I also see my stylist every week to make sure it looks as good as it can."

It's also important to craft your professional brand with your goals in mind, and to share them with the network you're building. Who do you want to be? Who will help you get there? Who's already there, and how did they get there? Younger professionals are eager to ask for mentorship, but it's important to understand exactly what you're seeking from the relationship. Are you looking for someone who will help you navigate through your company and speak on your behalf when there's a promotion available or a new project forming? You need a sponsor, either within your company or at the company you wish to join one day. Developing a relationship with a sponsor is a long-term effort, and you need to be clear about the value you offer to them as well. Whether it's understanding the idiosyncrasies of your generation or how your specific life experience informs how you approach your work, be sure to share them regularly.

Do you want someone to offer counsel on a frequent basis, or on whatever challenge you face instead? Find a coach with whom you have good chemistry and who has experience in helping other clients get to where they want to be. Are you looking for specific, situational advice? That's where actual mentors come in. In my experience, the most helpful mentors have been the ones who shared how they approached the specific situation I'd found myself in. If you're seeking a mentoring moment like this from someone who's extremely busy, offer a concise summary of the situation and two or three specific questions they can answer. Be flexible about how you hear from them, and suggest that they send you a voice memo or an email if their schedule is packed. Before you make the request, search for interviews or podcasts they may have done that might answer your question.

Some of my most valued advisers—like Vice President Harris—have no clue that they've mentored me over the years, and it makes for a memorable way to introduce yourself if you ever have the chance to meet them. When I met Vice President Harris, I mentioned the little notebook of her quotes that I had collected over the past seven years, and the strength and motivation they gave me in stressful times. She responded by giving me a hug, which may have been one of the best moments of my life.

No matter who you connect with—a sponsor, a coach, a mentor—follow up with them. Let them know how you approached a situation, or reach out after a conversation with some new thoughts, and let them know what you're up to. Following up and sharing updates gives them an opportunity to learn more about you and demonstrates your professionalism and follow-through.

BALANCING HUSTLE AND HUMILITY

Hustling on your ambition is important. Humility is equally important, though it is rarely talked about. There are going to be times in your career when you make mistakes, or the effects of your work have unintended consequences. There will also be times where your work is dissected under a microscope and things are taken out of context and blown up to fit a narrative. No one understands this better than Kamala. In every race she's run, her record as a prosecutor and an elected official has come under scrutiny, often far more than her opponents' records. Specific cases would be cherry-picked and told in a narrative meant to define Kamala one-dimensionally by her opponents. These narratives ignore context and timing of those cases, and the fact that candidates evolve on issues over time. As she transitioned from law enforcer to lawmaker, Kamala spoke more more publicly and humbly about her record, acknowledging where she could have done more or done things differently. She has also built relationships with some of her fiercest critics, listening to their perspective and shifting her position on various criminal justice issues in the past five years.

As a law enforcement official, Kamala walked the tightrope of being a Black woman and working in a system whose mandate was mass incarceration and justice was punitive. When she was assistant district attorney of Alameda County in 1992, the number of murders in Oakland reached a record high of 165. Her power as an assistant district attorney was limited, especially during her turn on "The Bridge," a division in the office that processed drug crimes by the hundreds.

Kamala's colleagues were quick to make charges based on appearances, not considering the details of the case. Details like what a defendant was wearing, what music he had in the car, or where he was picked up sometimes added the charge of gang enhancement. The more minor offenses—being under the influence in public, simple possession—had the book thrown at them. Kamala spoke up when she could. She butted into her colleagues' conversations, informing them that her family lived in those neighborhoods and dressed the same way. But she had a job to do, at the peak of a drug epidemic and in a "tough on crime" office.

San Francisco was not faring better when she was elected district attorney. In 2004, San Francisco County had the highest homicide rate in California with eighty-eight homicides reported (nineteen more than the year before). The Sunnydale housing projects were the target of an anti-gang injunction from the city attorney and RICO (Racketeer Influenced and Corrupt Organizations) actions from the federal government. The neighborhood was its most dangerous when Kamala was district attorney, yet she would venture to Sunnydale at night to host sessions that showed the reality of what gun violence and convictions would look like. In her first six months as district attorney, she cleared twenty-seven of the seventy-four backlogged homicide cases and took forty-nine violent crime cases to trial, securing thirty-six convictions. Her goal was to make San Francisco—and especially neighborhoods like Sunnydale—a safer place to live. Her approach was focused both inside and outside of the courtroom, in getting convictions and in getting to know the communities that were most affected.

In the past three decades, there has been a significant change in public sentiment on justice. In the 1990s, the issue was presented with only two options—being tough on crime or soft on crime. This approach did not factor in the realities of so many communities, where crime rates were higher but its residents were more likely to face excessive force. Racial profiling was the norm, and the impact on Black communities nationwide was severe. In certain neighborhoods, any crime was determined to be a serious crime simply because of where it happened or the color of the defendant's skin. Kamala became a prosecutor to change the system from within, but there were limits to what she could do as a prosecutor or district attorney. And in order to advance to a higher role to make greater change, she had to stay electable and retain the support of those who helped her win her election. This is not meant to be a blanket defense of her record, but to explain why she focused on certain issues (prosecute three-strike offenders in the case of violent felonies, never to seek the death penalty) and did not take a forceful stand on others (such as the legalization of cannabis or abolishing the death penalty).

One issue that tested Kamala's hustle and humility balance was truancy in California. While she was on assignment in juvenile court as assistant district attorney, truancy was widespread in Oakland schools and more than twenty thousand students in the school district tested below the 50th percentile. The district was so troubled that a trustee had been appointed to oversee its finances. As a prosecutor and district attorney, she knew that the vast majority of prisoners were high school dropouts. Back on Track focused on helping nonviolent, first-time offenders successfully reenter society. But why were so many high school dropouts—more than 80 percent—in prison to begin with?

Kamala learned the answer from superintendent Arlene Ackerman, who shared some sobering facts. A large number of the habitually truant high school students had also missed just as much school while they were in elementary school. At the time, the curriculum up to third grade had focused on teaching the students to read. From fourth grade onward, reading was a requirement to learn the curriculum. "If students can't read, they can't learn, and they fall further behind, month after month and year after year—which forces them onto a nearly inescapable path to poverty," Kamala wrote in her memoir. "You could map the path for children who started drifting away from the classroom when they were young. The truant child became the wanderer...who became the target for gang recruiters...who became the young drug courier... who became the perpetrator—or the victim—of violence."

The goal was never to lock up parents, though that was what was reported. Kamala wanted to end the cycle that filled San Francisco's jails and prisons. Addressing truancy was a way to do that, though her ability to do so as district attorney was limited. The program she launched as district attorney was broader and offered more services than is typically reported. The strict letters sent by her office got the most press, but the initiative included a series of meetings with habitually truant families and connecting them with community services to assist them in getting their children to school. Prosecution was a last resort, and there were only seven cases where parents were brought to court. Despite the unpopularity of the issue, Kamala's initiative was successful and reduced elementary school truancy by 23 percent over three years. She would go on to pursue a statewide initiative as attorney general, with a bill passed in the California State Legislature in 2010. In the following years, truancy rates dropped statewide by 4 percent. While these efforts were successful in reducing truancy, there were families who were still prosecuted by district attorneys and jailed as a result. When campaigning for president, Kamala answered the question on her truancy initiative honestly. "My regret is that I have now heard stories where, in some jurisdictions, DAs have criminalized the parents. And I regret that that has happened," she told Jon Favreau on Pod Save America. "And the thought that anything that I did could have led to that, because that certainly was not the intention—never was the intention. Never was the intention."

Some of Harris's harshest critics when she was district attorney and attorney general have credited her growth on criminal justice when she was elected to the Senate. She quietly met with activists like DeRay Mckesson and Rashad Robinson, where she answered for her previous actions openly and explained her rationale behind them. Kamala has continued to build relationships with them, and has shown progression on her approach to criminal justice that meets the time and circumstances of the past five years.

One of the first bills Kamala introduced as a senator was to reform cash bail in each state, a policy that disproportionally affects low-income Black people. She encouraged states to adopt systems that evaluated each person's flight risk and danger to the public. If both are low, a person should be released without any money being exchanged. She reached across the aisle and worked with Senator Rand Paul of Kentucky to co-sponsor this bill, which unfortunately never came to the floor for a vote. Kamala forged on and fought for the passage of an anti-lynching bill co-sponsored with Senators Tim Scott of South Carolina and Cory Booker of New Jersey. With Senator Booker, she also introduced the sweeping Justice in Policing Act, which called for limiting qualified immunity for police officers, creating a national misconduct registry, and banning choke holds.

Being humble is not a quality often associated with Kamala (rather, it's attributed more to President Joe Biden). Kamala's other qualities—confidence, assertiveness, ambition—are more commonly attributed to her. It's her balance of humility and hustle that I find inspiring, and this balance is something I've tried to cultivate myself. Shyamala cultivated humility early in everything she did as a mother. If Kamala or Maya attempted to earn praise for a small task, they'd immediately be called out. "Why would I applaud you for something you were supposed to do?" she'd respond. Being humble served Kamala well throughout her career. It kept her focused on programs like Back on Track when she was district attorney, and building solutions to address truancy within her powers as attorney general. Kamala's humility helped her evolve on her previous record and grow in public, apologizing and expressing regret for past actions and using her role as senator to introduce bolder plans for criminal justice.

So how does one cultivate humility? The word is defined as "the quality of having a modest or low view of one's importance." While I bristle at the definition, I attribute humility with knowing just how much you do *not* know, and confidently so. These days, this quality is known as a *growth mindset*. The concept was coined by psychologist Carol Dweck after spending two decades researching why some people rise to the occasion and blossom when facing challenges. Those with a *fixed mindset* give up quickly and appear to wilt in the same circumstances. "For twenty years, my research has shown that the view you adopt for yourself profoundly affects the way you lead your life," Dweck writes in *Mindset*. "It can determine whether you become the person you want to be and whether you accomplish the things you value. How does this happen? How can a simple belief have the power to transform your psychology and, as a result, your life?" Decades before the term was coined, Shyamala Gopalan was living a growth mindset when she landed in Berkeley to earn her PhD. Her mindset was strengthened by her active participation in the civil rights movement, and in marrying Donald Harris for love and later divorcing him when the relationship was no longer working.

Adopting a growth mindset is a choice. It's not enough to claim you have a growth mindset and continue to shy away from challenges or reject constructive feedback. One of the biggest hurdles in adopting a growth mindset is fixed-mindset triggers. There are internal and external triggers that push us into a fixed mindset, and identifying them is the first step to embracing a growth mindset. Think about the last time you snapped back at an offhand comment, or when you got defensive and a little hostile in a conversation. What was the topic? What was said that made you feel that way? Did you have any other thoughts before responding?

Commit to jotting down the moments you are defensive, snippy, or rigid over the course of a week. Make notes of what triggers you, and how you respond in the moment. At the end of the week, review the list and look for patterns. Did a casual remark push you to say something you regretted? Is there something in your home that set you off? What was it about that Instagram post that had you reeling, and why? By understanding why we react to the common things that set us off, we can teach ourselves to pause and process when we face them in the future.

There is great power in a pause. We're living in a time when we're constantly connected via multiple forms of communication. Responses are expected immediately, if not sooner. The power of statements is waning, as everyone flocks to social media to claim allegiance or denounce whatever is trending but rarely takes action on the issue at hand. Stepping back from the fray and giving yourself a moment to process what is happening, how it's making you feel, and how you wish to engage goes against the grain right now. It is easy to post a black square on your Instagram feed or fire off a response to an email seconds after you open it. We share articles on social media without reading them and verifying their accuracy first. We shout our opinions at the top of our lungs without listening to others', or unpacking our beliefs to see if they are in line with the truth. We do these things because it's what others are doing, and because it's simple.

Stepping back, processing, and responding thoughtfully goes against the always-on, loud-is-right, simplistic messaging that's become the norm. Pausing and processing is uncomfortable and challenging, and it's also where growth happens. So when you feel the need to rage tweet or briskly respond to an email, pause. Take a second to fully process what you're responding to. If something is unclear, respond with a question. Keep your tone professional and gracious. Will it take a little bit longer to come to a resolution? Perhaps. Will that resolution be more satisfying and considerate for everyone? It likely will. The more you pause and process before responding, the more others in your circle will take note. And maybe they'll start doing the same.

Identifying our fixed-mindset triggers and teaching ourselves new ways to react is uncomfortable. Teaching ourselves to listen and process rather than react when we hear something that seems negative or critical is emotionally and mentally taxing. But that's exactly how to live with a growth mindset. Get comfortable with being uncomfortable. Use your pause times to pick up a skill or hobby you've always wanted to do. I often spend my pauses picking up my latest needlepoint project, and find that stitching a row or section helps me formulate the right response or come up with another approach to a challenge. A quick walk outside clears my head in a way scrolling through Twitter or Instagram never has. Putting my phone away while I make a cup of tea gives me physical and mental distance from the problem I'm facing, and helps my emotions settle. While I have regretted some of the tweets I've sent or the way I've responded to an email, I have never once regretted a pause.

If this seems intimidating to you, start practicing pauses in just one area of your life. It could be your company's messaging platform or emails. It might be social media. Or it could be the uncomfortable conversations we find ourselves in with people who view issues differently than we do. Pick one of these things, and commit to practicing the pause with them. If you choose email, you might consider putting an auto-responder on your personal account informing people that you are being more intentional with your time and will respond when you've been able to properly process their message and write a thoughtful response. If you choose social media, pick a single platform to start with and be aggressive with muting or unfollowing the profiles that don't bring you value. Following accounts that you find yourself judging or disagreeing with—and promptly sharing their posts with your friends to comment on it further—will keep you stuck in your fixed mindset.

Ambition alone is not enough to succeed. It takes hustle and humility, and a great deal of it. You will have your critics and naysayers. "There will be a resistance to your ambition, there will be people who say to you 'you are out of your lane,'" Kamala told the attendees of the Black Girls Lead 2020 conference. "They are burdened by only having the capacity to see what has always been instead of what can be. But don't you let that burden you."

HOW TO BORROW RESILIENCE FROM YOUR ANCESTORS

by Komal Minhas

"You come from a long line of warriors." My great-uncle uttered these words to me a week before he passed as we sat in my ancestral home in Punjab, India. There he would recount to me our family history dating back three generations and share the hardships, successes, and times of rebuilding that our family had endured.

I recorded that interaction—thirty minutes or so of conversation and history that I didn't realize our family would cherish shortly thereafter.

Having grown up in northern Alberta, I never truly understood the deep connection to land that some have until that trip. It was there, in India, that I realized I belonged to something greater than myself. It was there that I was able to tap into a well of power and strength I didn't know I had access to.

As I consider my own resiliency, I realize so much of it is inherited and learned from those who came before me. When I consider the stories of my ancestors and the jagged paths they took and the choices they made, I realize how much of my strength is the strength of a collective. A collective I can't always see or make sense of, but a collective I can feel as I endure and overcome the challenges that life has offered me to overcome.

When I think of Kamala Harris and the resilient history coursing through her veins, I can't help but reflect on her lineage, ancestry, and the strength provided to her through the ether.

As you reflect on your inner strength and resiliency, I invite you to consider this question: How has my ancestry informed who I am today and how I show up in the face of adversity?

For some, this may be a difficult inquiry as you may not know your parents, let alone the generations prior, or you may be disconnected from your bloodline for various reasons. If that's you, consider the strength and resilience you've created for yourself. How have you crafted a life that supports you in the face of adversity? Or how would you like to?

Connecting to our identity and heritage, alongside assessing and building the community of support we have around us, are key ways to enhance our resiliency and capacity to show up in the face of trauma and hardship. You can borrow strength and courage from those you love and those who have come before you. I've done it time and time again. I've borrowed the courage of my maternal grandmother on her first day at college when she was the first woman in her family to attend. I've tapped into the strength of my father as he landed on Canadian soil in

1974 with a new language and life to explore. I've channeled my mother's resilience as she continued life after miscarriages and the sudden losses of both her sisters.

I imagine the same for the Harris women. A collective weaving of courageous acts and moments of resilience from the last many decades — a tapestry so strong it supports these powerful women to rise time and time again. For Kamala, it raised her up all the way to the White House.

As you face all that's ahead for you, I invite you to channel what has gotten you to this point in your life. And as you act, I ask you to consider the resilient ancestor you may become.

"Optimism is the fuel driving every fight I've been in."

CHAPTER 4

Focus on Your North Star

It was a sunny, warm day in Oakland on January 28, 2019. Twenty thousand people had gathered to hear Senator Kamala Harris announce her candidacy for president of the United States. The crowd's chanting of "Ka-ma-la! Ka-ma-la!" drowned out Mary J. Blige's "Work That" as the senator took the stage, beaming and waving. Once the crowd settled down, she launched into her speech. She shared the story of her parents and how they made their way to Northern California, that she was born just down the street at Kaiser Hospital, and that her career began in Oakland.

"It was just a couple blocks from this very spot that nearly thirty years ago as a young district attorney I walked into the courtroom for the very first time and said the five words that would guide my life's work:

"'Kamala Harris, for the people.'

"…my whole life, I've only had one client: the people."

"For the people" is more than Kamala's presidential campaign slogan, or a common refrain in her speeches. It's been her North Star from the early days of her career as a prosecutor. "'For the people' was my compass—and there was nothing I took more seriously than the power I possessed," Kamala wrote in her memoir. "As an individual prosecutor, I had the discretion to decide whether to bring charges against someone and, if so, what and how many charges to bring…I was just starting out as a prosecutor, and yet I had the power to deprive a person of their liberty with the swipe of my pen."

When Kamala was prosecuting sex crimes, the people she fought for were the victims—often young girls and boys—who had suffered unspeakable abuse, often at the hands of people they once trusted. She kept these children top of mind as she spearheaded the safe house for youth sex workers at the city attorney's office in San Francisco. The young men she met in her first visit to county jail, mostly Black and Brown and low-income, were top of mind as she developed Back on Track. And when she was sworn in as attorney general, the tens of thousands of Californians who lost their homes to fore-closure were the people she was focused on helping.

In 2011, the mortgage crisis was at its peak, with homeowners lining up at their banks pleading for refinancing or modifications to keep their homes. Californians would come to her events with overflowing files with their mortgage paperwork, begging for her help. At a roundtable with victims of foreclosure, Denise Collins wiped her tears and put her glasses on before apologizing for crying and saying, "It's just a house." She spoke of purchasing her first home in Bayview in 1997, remarking how much she loved the neighborhood and San Francisco, and how it had become her home after moving from Southern California. Twelve years later, she had fallen behind on her mortgage payments by one month and, despite her being in the midst of a loan modification process, was informed that her home would be foreclosed on Monday. She was told the Friday before, at 3:45 p.m. Denise lost her home and declared bankruptcy. "I am completely destitute because of it," she told the roundtable. "That's my story...and that's why I contacted Kamala Harris, because at that point, I had nowhere else to go."

In 2011, the settlement between the justice departments

and the banks on the mortgage crisis looked like a done deal. Homeowners who declared bankruptcy would receive a small check in exchange for the banks being granted immunity from future claims and crimes that may have been committed. Kamala walked away from the negotiations and the Mortgage Fraud Strike Force launched investigations into Fannie Mae and Freddie Mac (which owned more than half of the mortgages under dispute) and the mortgage-backed securities that were sold to the California public employee pension fund. The task force also investigated instances of robo-signing—the automatic signatures of foreclosure documents that were not inspected or reviewed—which exacerbated the foreclosure crisis in both California and the country at large.

Friends and consultants warned Kamala that the banks would spend millions against her reelection. "I hope you know what you're doing," warned her predecessor and then-governor Jerry Brown. Even the White House and federal Department of Justice were trying to bring her back into settlement negotiations. Kamala stood firm, focused on the people she served. She spent the next months working with Beau Biden, Delaware's attorney general, who had joined her cause and had launched his own investigation. And every night before bed, she prayed, "God, please help me do the right thing."

In the months that passed, Kamala gained two more attorneys general for her fight, Martha Coakley and Catherine Cortez-Masto (from Massachusetts and Nevada, respectively). Kamala and her team kept flying back and forth to Washington, DC, for discussions with the banks. They weren't willing to budge from their original settlement offer, and neither were Kamala and her allies. The months stretched into a new year. In January, after one of her colleagues had just hung up with JPMorgan's counsel, Kamala made a call. "Get me Jamie Dimon," she said, taking off her earrings as she was transferred to JPMorgan's chairman and CEO. After shots were fired—"You're trying to steal from my shareholders!" "*My* shareholders are the homeowners of California! Talk to them about who got robbed!"—they got down to the details. Kamala presented her demands and walked Dimon through the details directly. He promised to speak with his board, and hung up the phone.

Two weeks later, California's settlement from the five largest banks was $18 billion, and would grow to $20 billion with additional settlements. Harris followed up the settlement with the California Bill of Rights, which would extend the protections from the foreclosure crisis beyond the three-year term and allow homeowners to sue when banks violated the new policies. The bill had little support from either side of the aisle, but Kamala would not be swayed. She and her team spent weeks in the Capitol, speaking with lawmakers one-on-one and slowly earning votes. When the bill came to the floor for a vote, Speaker John Pérez vowed to keep the vote open as long as he could so Kamala could convince legislators to switch their abstentions to yes votes. The bill passed both houses and was signed into law by the governor. California state senator Mark Leno credits Kamala with the success. "She made it happen," he told Dan Morian. "The whole game changed when Kamala got involved. The attorney general was not going to not get her way." Kamala took on the world's largest banks, the White House and the Justice Department, and her own colleagues to fight for the people. And she succeeded.

It's one thing to proclaim your North Star. It's quite another to live it. "Outcomes over optics" is the North Star of Nathalie Molina Niño, investor and author of *Leapfrog: The New Revolution for Women Entrepreneurs.* Her goal in life is to improve the lives of women at scale. Every startup she funds, every op-ed she writes, and every speech she gives is in service of that goal. But what you see is just the tip of the iceberg. Nathalie's public work pales in comparison to what she does quietly behind the scenes. For every editorial she's penned, she helps place at least two for other people whose message needs to be heard. She passes on speaking engagements to new voices, and supports them as they learn. "This isn't about delegation," Molina Niño told me. "*Outcomes over optics* is about centering what you want to see happen in the world first, then building/joining the army of geniuses best positioned to make it so. Sometimes the best thing you can do to get things done is pass the mic to the better voice." Outcomes over optics is the long game, and it's about rejecting the false narrative that you must dim your light in order to make room for others. This concept is known as Shine Theory (coined by Ann Friedman and Aminatou Sow), and it is a practice that's designed to uplift through collaboration rather than competition and false choices. If the goal is to make an impact and get things done, then outcomes trump optics every time.

If you don't have a phrase that defines your purpose and mission in life, you're not alone. I have struggled to find the pithy words that sum up what I want to achieve in this life, and I've given up on finding them. In *Drop the Ball,* Tiffany Dufu advises the reader to find their purpose by imagining what will be written on their tombstone. The exercise is to help you identify the things you do that serve these words, and drop the ball on tasks that do not. For Dufu, her life's work is advancing women and girls, and every decision she makes is in service of this.

"Everything that I have ever done is connected to women and girls in some way, like literally every job that I've had," said Dufu. "What I love is that I have this passion and this purpose and I execute whatever needs to happen at the time, so right now I have what I would call a 'portfolio career,' which I think is the future of work." Her portfolio career is being an entrepreneur, author, public speaker, and nonprofit board member. As the founder and CEO of the Cru, she has created a powerful platform for women, offering community through small group coaching and mentoring. In order to serve the larger vision, Dufu is surgical about the smaller decisions we often take for granted. Each of her meetings is exactly forty-five minutes, and she only accepts invitations when she has a specific role to play in the discussion. She brings this same energy to her personal life. Her goal as a mother is to raise conscious global citizens, which means she focuses on engaging in thoughtful conversations today. She'll ask her kids about the day they created for themselves or who they laughed with. These conversations are a priority for her, while her kids' social calendar is not (her husband manages it). By living up to her own standards, Dufu abandons the expectations that are often put on us. Living a life that aligns with your values and your purpose is something all of us should strive for, and it starts with knowing what we want written on our tombstone or in our obituary.

My North Star/epitaph lacks the brevity of Kamala and Nathalie's and the fortitude of Tiffany's, but I come back to it time and time again: My goal is to help women save time and energy on the things they have to do, so they have more time and energy for the things they want to do. My first book, *How to Pack: Travel Smart for Any Trip,* helped women tackle the dreaded task of packing and made it easier, faster, and more joyful. Hitha on the Go, the blog I began writing in 2009, was the launchpad for the book and packing more efficiently, but it also offered simple recipes that are incredibly flavorful, work-appropriate outfits at accessible price points, and tactics to work more productively. I created #5SmartReads to help people be more informed about what's happening, without being stressed out by the state of the world. I invest in companies that share this vision.

Most important, I claim my free time with joy and fill it with the things I love to do: read books, needlepoint, browse through cookbooks and cook a new dish, wander through the city or a museum with no agenda. Helping you save time and energy on the things you have to do is something I am good at and feel passionate about, but it's also because I'm all the more passionate about maximizing the time for me to do as I please.

I still say yes to meetings I don't need to attend and emails go unanswered despite my best efforts. My work often requires a recalibration where I reschedule calls and clear days from my calendar to get caught up on everything. During those weeks, I make it a point to write "save time and energy" on a Post-it and stick it on my laptop or desk to remind me of my North Star. Will this meeting/task/email/call help me save time and energy, or help others do the same? If the task needs to get done but doesn't serve this goal, is there someone I can delegate it to? Running every decision through this filter can seem counterproductive, but it's important if things have started to slip through that don't serve your mission.

BUILD RESILIENCE

St. Mary's Cathedral was packed on April 16, 2004. The church was filled with police officers, elected officials, and family and friends of Officer Isaac Espinoza, who was murdered the week before while patrolling the Bayview neighborhood of San Francisco. He was the first officer killed on duty in San Francisco in more than ten years. The mood in the chapel was mournful, but it was also tense during the eulogies. Senator Dianne Feinstein abandoned her prepared remarks and spoke forcefully. "This is not only the definition of tragedy, it's the special circumstance called for by the death penalty law," she declared. Most of the room stood clapping. One mourner remained seated in the front pew, her face stoic. Days before the funeral, Kamala Harris had charged the case as a special circumstance homicide, which carried a life sentence in prison with no possibility of parole. The reaction was swift and brutal.

"We, the command staff of this department, urge in the strongest possible terms that this capital murder case be prosecuted to the fullest extent, and that the death penalty be sought upon conviction, as permitted by law," declared Heather Fong, the chief of San Francisco's police force. More than forty members of

California's state assembly signed a resolution urging attorney general Bill Lockyer to investigate and intervene in the case. Police officers literally turned their backs on Kamala as she passed them in the Hall of Justice. For much of the law enforcement community, Kamala's sentence of life in prison was not the justice they envisioned.

She remained steadfast in her decision to not call for the death penalty. In an op-ed published in the *San Francisco Chronicle,* Kamala wrote, "For those who want this defendant put to death, let me say simply that there can be no exception to principle. I gave my word to the people of San Francisco that I oppose the death penalty and I will honor that commitment despite the strong emotions evoked by this case. I have heard and considered those pleas very carefully and I understand and share the pain that drives them, but my decision is made and it is final."

Not calling for the death penalty in Officer Espinoza's killing would follow Kamala for the rest of her career, igniting ire and support in equal measure. She was never again endorsed by the San Francisco Police Officers Association, and the relationship between the police department and the district attorney's office was strained for some time. Her decision, and her stance on the death penalty, would come up again six years later, as she ran for attorney general of California. Her opponent in the general election was Stephen Cooley, the district attorney of Los Angeles for the previous ten years. Unlike Kamala, he was publicly supportive on the death penalty. He earned the endorsement of nearly every newspaper in California. More important, he also had the endorsement of Officer Espinoza's widow and parents, and police unions invested $1.5 million to help elect him. The Republican State Leadership Committee even stepped in with a $1 million ad buy where Isaac Espinoza's widow, Renata, criticized Kamala for not seeking the death penalty. The race was considered a long shot for Kamala, but she was undeterred.

There was a single debate for California's attorney general race. On October 5, 2010, the candidates met at UC Davis and quickly traded fire over Proposition 8 (a ballot proposition to ban same-sex marriage), climate change policies, and the death penalty. But it was the *San Francisco Chronicle*'s Jack Leonard's question that would turn the tide of the race. He asked Cooley if he planned to collect his pension on top of the attorney general's salary, if elected. His annual pension was an estimated $300,000, on top of the $150,000 salary of the attorney general. Cooley responded, "Yes, I do. I earned it. Thirty-eight years of public service. I definitely earned whatever pension rights I have, and I will certainly rely upon that, as to supplement the very low, incredibly low salary that's paid to the state attorney general."

Kamala responded with a laugh, saying, "Go for it, Steve. You've earned it, there's no question." Her campaign quickly cut an ad with Cooley's words from the debate, closing with the text, "$150,000 a year isn't enough?" The ad ran in Los Angeles. The campaign followed the ad with a powerful endorsement from President Barack Obama, ten days before the election. Kamala had been one of his earliest supporters, hosting a fundraiser for him in the Bay Area when he was running for the US Senate, and an early endorser for his presidential run. Obama returned the favor and appeared at a rally at the University of Southern California, which was Cooley's law school alma mater. Despite the last polls still showing Cooley up by five, the race was too close to call. It would be another three weeks before every vote was counted and the election went to Kamala Harris, who won by 74,157 votes.

The death penalty continued to come up during

Kamala's tenure as attorney general. She was noticeably absent when death penalty repeals were ballot measures and her supporters expected her to publicly support them. "She said it came down to her role as an attorney general whose duties [included] writing the title and summary for state propositions," wrote John Diaz in the *San Francisco Chronicle*. "She wanted to avoid the perception of a potential conflict as both advocate and arbiter of ballot language." In the interview, she shared her personal vote to repeal the death penalty, but it did not satisfy her critics on the left.

A more challenging case drew further criticism on her position on the death penalty. In 2015, a federal district court judge had ruled that the delay of a murder-rapist's death penalty charge was "cruel and unusual punishment." Death penalty abolitionists expected Kamala to use this case to formally agree that the death penalty was unconstitutional, as she had done in the past. In the case of Proposition 8 (the ban on same-sex marriage), she agreed that Prop 8 was unconstitutional and passed on defending it. Kamala did appeal the death row case, citing her disagreement with the judge claiming that the cases took too long between conviction and execution. As attorney general, the Department of Corrections was her client. Although Kamala was correct from a legal perspective, the outrage was palpable and she confessed that it was one of the most difficult things she had to do.

It's one thing to stand for something when it's popular or convenient for your goals. It's quite another when you take heat for it from different people—especially when those people are powerful or gunning for your job. Kamala has always been consistent in regard to the death penalty, staying true to her North Star. "For the people" was why she refused to call for the death penalty, but also why she appealed in the 2015 case. As district attorney of San Francisco and attorney general of California, it was her job to administer justice for every resident in her city and state, respectively. Kamala's focus on her North Star and her resilience helped her through these difficult moments in her career. Resilience is one of those qualities that can't be learned from a book or a lecture. It is forged through experience that you live and observe.

Kamala's first lessons in resilience were watching her mother navigate the hierarchical, political world of academic research. Shyamala would advance to the final rounds of jobs simply so the grant writers could claim they considered a woman for the position, and dealt with chauvinist, demeaning men on a regular basis at work. Despite all of this, Shyamala was sought out by labs at the

University of Illinois and the University of Wisconsin, and was offered tenure at McGill University in Montreal before returning to Lawrence Berkeley. "She was a woman who, many times, people would overlook or not take her seriously. Or because of her accent, assume things about her intelligence," Harris said of her mother. "Now, every time, my mother proved them wrong."

Shyamala may have modeled and instilled resilience in her daughters through her actions, but it is a quality each of us can and should cultivate on our own. One of Shyamala's common refrains was "Don't let anyone tell you who you are; you tell them who you are." One important quality of resilience is reframing negative thoughts, which we absorb both consciously and subconsciously. How do you rewire your brain to stop absorbing microaggressions, negative comments, and the narratives that we accept as truth even though they feel wrong? You talk to yourself.

I stumbled across this advice on an episode of Kara Loewentheil's UnF*ck Your Brain podcast. She dedicated the entire episode to the secret of Dr. James Gills's success. I hadn't heard of him before listening, but quickly learned that Dr. Gills is an ocular surgeon who has performed the most lens implant and cataract surgeries in the world. He's also an author who distributes forty thousand free copies of his books in prisons every month. And he's completed six double Ironman triathlons, the most recent one completed when he was in his fifties. When asked about the secret to his success, he said, "I talk to myself more than I listen to myself."

Talking to yourself more than you listen to yourself is such a simple practice, but one of the most powerful practices you can do. It's something I do throughout the day, starting with talking myself through my entire morning routine ("you will get out of bed, you will make the bed right away, you will go brush your teeth"). Some mornings, these three activities are all I manage to do before my kids come barreling into the room and the day begins. As I sit at my desk in the morning, ready to tackle the day, I tell myself that I am smart, that I am a good communicator, that I solve problems, that I'm a strong leader, that I'm a good writer. I tell myself that I'm a good mother multiple times in the day, when my children are being especially willful. And anytime a negative, nonconstructive comment makes its way through an email or an Instagram comment or a direct message, I tell myself that I take care to share information clearly and honestly, that I only share what I am comfortable sharing, and that I am not everyone's cup of tea and that is more than okay.

Talking to yourself also helps strengthen other qualities of resilience, such as gratitude, reframing negative thoughts, and getting through hard moments. I tell myself the many things I'm grateful for throughout the day, from the cup of coffee I sip every morning to reminding myself that I get to do the work I do. Not a day goes by where I don't give thanks to the many privileges I have been born and raised with, and expressing gratitude for them reminds me to use them in service of others. Talking to yourself helps you get through the days where everything feels like it's going wrong and it all feels like a mess. Tell yourself that it is not just okay, but absolutely necessary to take some time to yourself and get some space from what's troubling you. Follow up those words with meaningful actions, whether it's climbing back in bed for a nap or treating yourself to a favorite meal. If you give yourself some space in this moment, you'll be able to rebound faster. And taking space starts with telling yourself to claim it for yourself.

Resilience is a muscle, and it requires regular exercise. The challenges you face will change as you grow older or take on new roles in your life. There are going to be many times where you don't know how you're going to do something. Focus on your North Star. Heed Shyamala's words and tell yourself who you are.

HOW TO FIND YOUR NORTH STAR

by Rachel Cantor

When I was in third grade, my whole world was dance.
I was auditioning for a competitive hip-hop dance
team and I dreamed of making new friends and
dancing my heart out on stage. The only problem: I
didn't think I would make the team.

My grandpa called to wish me luck, and introduced
me to the acronym PMA (Positive Mental Attitude)
and the power of positive thinking. He said that if I
believed in myself, knew that I did everything in my
power to prepare for the audition, I would do great
and probably make the team.

I immediately took out a piece of chalk and wrote
the letters *PMA* across my whole driveway. And ever
since that audition in third grade, I've written *PMA*
across the top of every test or quiz I've taken. It's
become a way for me to channel positivity and
remind myself "I got this." If I was nervous for an
exam, I would write *PMA* at least ten times across the
top of it. If I felt confident, a single eighteen-point
PMA across the top of the page would do the trick.
The acronym stuck with me from elementary school

all the way through college. Some of my middle school teachers called me "Miss PMA." Soon enough, it became my life mantra.

It used to be that I couldn't write a single paper without worrying about the grade, what my teacher would think, or if my writing skills were properly displayed. I couldn't solve a math problem without doubting my process and answer, but with a positive attitude, over the years, I learned to rise to the occasion, take on challenges, and believe in myself.

Three syllables, one acronym paused my self-competing marathon. Now when my inner critic talks, my blood quiets it and my hand automatically writes *PMA*.

Like Norman Peale's quote, "Change your thoughts, and you change your world," I was in the passenger seat as my family, friends, and teachers watched my positive attitude change my life. I gained the confidence to be the true me and follow my heart.

"Everything else can be crazy, I can be on six planes in one week, and what makes me feel normal is making Sunday night family dinner. If I'm cooking, I feel like I'm in control of my life."

CHAPTER 5

Eat *No* for Breakfast (And Take Care of Yourself)

When asked how she deals with rejection, Kamala said, "You know, I have in my career been told many times, 'It's not your time. It's not your turn. And let me just tell you, I eat 'no' for breakfast, so I would recommend the same. It's a hearty breakfast."

No can be intimidating. Those two small letters evoke big emotions: rejection, disappointment, even failure. We are more likely to remember all the times we've been told *no* than the times we've been told *yes*. We remember the jobs we didn't get, the promotions or raises that remained out of reach, the negative things we overheard people saying about us. Judgments from others may not sting as quickly as rejections do, but they can take root in our minds and change the way we see and know ourselves. If you hear the same thing about yourself over and over again, at what point do you begin to believe it?

Kamala Harris knows how to deal with naysayers and judgmental people alike. In her first election for district attorney of San Francisco, her candidacy was considered a long shot. Fellow challenger Bill Fazio and sitting DA Terence Hallinan were well financed, won the coveted endorsements, and had the name recognition in the community. Kamala was polling at 6 percent and had a campaign headquarters in Bayview, a working-class, diverse neighborhood in southeast San Francisco. She also had something that neither of her opponents had: an ironing board in her car. When she wasn't knocking on doors or standing at bus stops to introduce herself to San Francisco voters, she'd set up the ironing board at grocery stores, tape her campaign posters around it, and hand out her campaign fliers and speak to everyone who passed by. She turned the "no one knew who Kamala Harris was" *no* into a multipronged effort to introduce herself through campaigning and direct mail, eventually winning the coveted endorsement from the *San Francisco Chronicle*.

Rather than focus on the naysayers, Kamala focused on the people she would serve and made her case to them. As much as she preferred to discuss policy and her positions on the issues, the voters wanted to know more about her. Talking about herself did not come naturally to Kamala, as her mother had taught her and her sister that talking about oneself was vain and to focus on action instead. In this instance, the action was to tell her future constituents about herself—and so she did. While this outreach moved the needle slightly in terms of name recognition, it taught her the importance of showing up, sharing her story, and asking for support. It had to be earned, and she worked to earn it.

It's one thing to get out there and flip the *no*s based on not knowing. It's quite another to deal with *no*s based on judgments formed by others, which Kamala deftly did in her first debate in her first DA race. Her previous romantic relationship with former mayor Willie Brown had always been common knowledge, but the two appointments he granted her were coming under scrutiny and amplified by her opponents. Brown still wielded significant influence in San Francisco politics, having supported future governor Gavin Newsom and other rising stars with similar appointments, and supporting both Newsom and Kamala in the 2002 citywide elections. When a voter asked Kamala if she could operate independently of her former partner's influence in the city's politics, she swiftly dismissed the question and went on offense about her opponents' own questionable attacks on each other. Then she focused on the audience. "I want to make a commitment to you that my campaign is not going to be about negative attacks. I believe we need to talk about the issues and the policies and the way we're going to move our criminal justice system forward." When Fazio attempted to respond with a mailer bringing up Kamala's appointments to various committees by Brown, she responded with a recorded phone call where she addressed the appointments succinctly. While we don't know how many voters that call swayed, it did help her make the runoff election, which she went on to win.

Kamala's approach to dealing with judgment—address, dismiss, and go on offense—is formidable. It was cultivated in her time as a prosecutor, strengthened through her subsequent campaigns and serving on the Senate Judiciary Committee, and has prepared her for the situations she'll face as vice president and beyond. However, it's not the only approach to deal with judgment. There are several, but they all start with one common trait—bravery. Bravery is not a finite resource that we're born with. It's a choice we must make in every difficult moment, a practice we must invest in every day, and a journey with no finish line. Bravery begets bravery; the more you practice and work at it, the braver you'll be and the easier you'll find it to be brave.

Harris's bravery is how she owns her multitudes, takes action, and eats *no* for breakfast every morning. Her bravery muscles must have superhuman strength by now because she has put in decades of practice.

So how does one practice bravery? It starts with unlearning what we've been taught and have been molded into since we were young. "Boys are taught to be brave, while girls are taught to be perfect." Reshma Saujani shared this revelatory truth, and it's one she came to through her work as the founder and CEO of Girls Who Code (and as a failed candidate for US Congress and public advocate for New York City). Our bravery muscles are weak from not being used enough, while our minds and bodies are exhausted from living up to the high standards that are set for us and the higher ones we set for ourselves. Practicing bravery starts with taking care of yourself, which we'll discuss in a bit.

It also requires you to embrace the power of "yet," as Saujani recommends. Adding "yet" to the things you tell yourself about you ("I'm not strong" to "I'm not strong...yet") can be easier than embracing positive affirmations as we start to rebuild our bravery muscles. In time, those positive affirmations ("I am strong, I am wise, I am important") will become easier to say and believe, especially as you borrow confidence from those who see your truth. But if these phrases seem a little scary, start with "yet."

Asking for feedback is an excellent way to build your bravery. It was a key tenet of the training I received in Cisco's Sales Associates Program, and drilled into us to ask after every practice sales call, presentation, and evaluation with our managers. Asking for feedback works several of your mental muscles at the same time. On the surface, feedback shows you where and how you can improve. More important, it teaches you how to filter constructive criticism from judgment. There is a fine line between the two, and it often blurs in the context of formal evaluations like performance reviews or presentations. In asking for feedback regularly, you'll train your ear to focus on the helpful ways you can improve, and let the personal opinions float out the other ear. Asking for feedback should not be limited to professional efforts alone. Ask your friends or your partner how you can better support them, if "How have I been as a friend/ partner?" is too intimidating. Asking the children in your life for their feedback is a humbling and hilarious experience, making it a great starting point. "Inviting criticism enables you to bear witness to your own imperfections and build a tolerance for them. First tolerance, then acceptance, and then, believe it or not, joy," says Saujani.

Eating *no* for breakfast is an acquired taste. It can take some time before the rejections and judgments of others stop tasting bitter and your bravery muscles start feeling strong. This is where self-care comes in, but not the Instagrammable face-mask-cozy-robe-filtered perfection that comes to mind when you hear those words. It's about taking care of yourself, oxygen-mask-in-airplane style.

TAKING CARE OF YOURSELF

Kamala practices nonnegotiable self-care daily, starting with a morning workout no matter what. "It's about your mind. I work out every morning. Only half an hour. I get on the treadmill. That's it. Every morning, I don't care what time. It gets your blood flowing. It gets your adrenaline flowing." True to form, she had just returned from a walk with her husband when she got the news that the election had been called for Joe Biden and her. "We did it, Joe. We did it. You're going to be president," she gleefully said into the phone, clad in leggings and a pullover. Talk about an endorphin rush.

Eating well is Harris's other nonnegotiable. Her day begins with raisin bran in almond milk and hot tea with lemon and honey. Her meals are filled with vegetables, whether it's a salad made with leftover roast chicken from the previous night's dinner or adding extra celery, onion, and herbs in a quick tuna salad sandwich that had been a staple during COVID-19 quarantine. Her meals are often made with the herbs from her garden, and she maximizes every meal she can. The carcass from the roast chicken will be used to make broth for a batch of soup. When Harris is on the road, she seeks out local restaurants for healthier options, and also to find community and connect with others.

No day is the same for Harris, but there is a comfort in starting every day the same way through her morning routine. The simpler something is, the easier it is to stick with it. But how do you figure out what to prioritize, and how to fit it in? There is no perfect routine or self-care ritual that fulfills all of us, but there are guidelines to help you find yours. Investor and entrepreneur Randi Zuckerberg's Pick Three framework challenges you to choose just three things each day—such as work, family, friends, sleep, or fitness—and do them to the best of your ability. Pick Three allows you to adjust your focus based on each day. If you're under the weather but have a tight deadline, you'll pick sleep, work, and family. Got a sick kid? Family is your priority, but you may be able to fit in sleep and fitness while your little one rests. Pick Three is a helpful starting point, especially when you're in the discovery phase of your self-care routine. The beauty of Pick Three is that you don't have to pick nor do the same things every day. Each day brings its own priorities and possibilities to try new things. Keep a running list on your phone of all the things that you'd like to eventually try in Work, Play, Family, and Fitness, but also have a list of tried-and-true things that you can fall back on when you're too tired or overwhelmed to decide what workout to do or what to work on first.

In this chapter of her life, it appears that Kamala's three things are fitness, work, and family (and they will change in the future). She treats her morning workouts with the same seriousness she brings to her job, and the same care she brings to her marriage and relationships with her family. Work and family are two permanent picks on my list, and I alternate sleep and fitness depending on how I'm feeling. Since work and family require most of my energy and decision-making power, I keep things very simple on the sleep and exercise fronts. On the days I prioritize sleep, I put my phone on airplane mode at nine p.m., take a warm bath, and read a "security blanket" book (the old favorites you keep coming back to when you want something familiar). I have certain pajamas for early bedtime nights to make them a little more special, and I listen to soothing music as I finish my last chapter and go to sleep.

If I'm committing to fitness one day, I set out my workout clothes the night before and will reach for a coordinated set that makes me want to break out a sweat. There are three workouts I truly love—indoor cycling, yoga, and dance—so I'll pick a video from each category and have them queued up on my tablet. Come morning, when I've made my bed and gotten changed into my workout clothes, I'll decide which type of workout I'm feeling like and jump straight into it. These little hacks, along with having set breakfasts and lunches, help me reduce decision fatigue.

"Decision fatigue" is more than a buzzy term you find in a business magazine. "It's a state of low will-power that results from having invested effort into making choices," said Roy Baumeister, a psychology professor at Florida State University who coined the term in 2010. "It leads to putting less effort into making further choices, so either choices are avoided or they are made in a very superficial way." Every little decision you make—from what you choose to wear to what you eat for breakfast to what show you decide to watch at night—chips away at your willpower. The more energy you put into these seemingly small decisions, the less willpower you'll have when you're faced with more pressing decisions. Kamala Harris minimizes her decisions in her mornings. Her morning routine is getting in thirty minutes of cardio, eating the same breakfast, and dressing in a suit or simple separates. Maintaining this routine every day lets her brain default to heuristics (or mental shortcuts) and conserve her energy and willpower for more pressing decisions.

Think about the decisions you make every day. Are there any where you would be fine with the same one or two options? On days when my kids are still sleeping, I start every single day with a ten-minute guided meditation that my smart speaker plays while I'm still in bed, and then a ten-minute yoga flow (which I select every Sunday, and do every day that week). I added Kamala's go-to breakfast to my rotation (store-brand raisin bran with almond milk), or a green smoothie (spinach, banana, protein powder, almond milk, and peanut butter), or sourdough toasted with cream cheese and mango chutney. I dress from the power piece section of my closet every morning (more about that in Chapter 6). I opt for salad for lunch most days, and pick one from my three favorites. I realize that these make me sound like the most boring person alive, but having default decisions allows me to expend my mental energy on negotiating with vendors, or writing thousands of words a day, or helping calm down one of my kids. By conserving my willpower and energy on the many tiny decisions I have to make, I have more for the big things that require my full self.

YOUR SACRED RITUALS

It's one thing to do certain things because they're good for you, like exercising, eating healthy, and getting a reasonable amount of sleep. But self-care isn't limited to the things we do to stay healthy. It's also about investing in the things that bring us happiness. And few things make Kamala happier than cooking.

"Kamala, you clearly like to eat good food. You better learn how to cook," Shyamala told her elder daughter, brandishing the cleaver in her hand as she chopped vegetables. The kitchen was the heart of the Harris home, with cabinets filled with fragrant spices housed in recycled Taster's Choice jars and the scent of freshly baked cookies wafting through the air. The girls grew up eating traditional South Indian favorites like dosa and potato curry or Kamala's favorite, idli. They also enjoyed the results of Shyamala's cooking experiments, from oyster beef stew to the different sandwiches she'd prepare for their school lunches. While most kids tucked into their bologna or PB&J, the Harris girls enjoyed cream cheese with olives on dark rye.

Meals were sacred in the Harris household. Shyamala was an early adopter of meal prepping on the weekends, well before the term was coined. Aretha Franklin would play as Shyamala cooked, with Kamala and Maya singing and dancing in the living room. Leftovers were presented as smorgasbord—bread cut in shapes from cookie cutters and served alongside pickles, mustard, mayonnaise, and whatever the previous night's dinner was. Bad days were turned around with "unbirthday parties," complete with cake and presents.

Harris found a home in Regina Shelton's kitchen as well, savoring the Southern specialties Mrs. Shelton always had on hand. Harris savored her pound cake and biscuits, and it was Mrs. Shelton she wanted to impress with one of her early baking attempts. She had made lemon bars by herself, finding the recipe in her mother's cookbooks, carefully measuring all the ingredients and mixing them together, and cutting the cooled bars and arranging them on a plate. Harris brought the bars to Mrs. Shelton, who was enjoying the afternoon with Shyamala and other friends. "Mmmm, honey. That's delicious…maybe a little too much salt…but really delicious," Mrs. Shelton replied after taking a large bite. Harris had mistakenly used salt instead of sugar, but

Mrs. Shelton's warm response and gentle correction built up her confidence in the kitchen, and in life.

Kamala's passion for cooking and food only grew with her. Her niece Meena recalls that "Kamala especially is the type of person where you ask her one question [about cooking] and then she's like, 'Oh! Let me tell you…' and then you're on the phone with her for like two hours and then she follows up via email with sixteen recipes that you did not ask for and then she follows up: 'Did you make it? How did it turn out? Did you do this? Did you make sure to do it this way?'" Cooking is one of Harris's treasured rituals. Her eyes light up and she becomes animated when asked how to brine a turkey or teaching Senator Warner how to make tuna salad sandwiches over Instagram Live. She reads *The New York Times* cooking app and cookbooks to unwind (*Jubilee* by Toni Tipton-Martin is a favorite). She talks lovingly about the cilantro rice she ate at Sabrina's West Street Kitchen in Reno and shared her concern for Sabrina's business during the coronavirus pandemic, wondering if she was able to secure any funds from the relief program. Politics has always been personal for Harris, but it's especially evident when she is talking about food.

There is one ritual where politics and work take a backseat to the food, and that's Sunday night dinner. It's a beloved tradition in the Harris–Emhoff household, one that began when she and Doug were engaged. Harris plans the meal from her cookbooks and apps the week before, and begins prepping the meal on Friday or Saturday. The family then comes together on Sunday to prepare the meal. While Emhoff dons his onion goggles and chops the vegetables, Harris's stepdaughter Ella prepares guacamole and the dessert. Stepson Cole takes care of setting the table and selecting the playlist, and pitches in as sous chef. Harris focuses on the main dish, which is as varied as her mother's own kitchen experiments. Dinner may be biryani, or chicken prepared with feta, lemon, and oregano. If it's been a travel-heavy week, Harris opts for tacos or another simple meal. The family sits at the table and savors the meal together.

"I know not everyone likes to cook, but it's centering for me. And as long as I'm making Sunday family dinner, I know I'm in control of my life—doing something that matters for the people I love, so we can share that quality time together," Kamala has said. For her, Sunday family dinners are more than just a meal or a family tradition. In *The Power of Ritual,* Casper ter Kuile talks about transforming the habits and routines in our lives into a meaningful practice that strengthens our connection across four levels: with ourselves, those around us, the natural world, and the transcendent. For Kamala, cooking is exactly that.

The time she spends planning the meal and gathering ingredients throughout the week is a way to connect with herself. The actual meal—both cooking and enjoying it—is done with her family, a chance to reconnect every week. Going out into her garden and gathering herbs is her way of connecting with the natural world. The entire ritual is a way for her to connect with her late mother, given how sacred mealtimes were for Shyamala and the girls when they were young. Family dinner is more than a tradition or even a ritual; it's part of her *Rule of Life*. Ter Kuile defines the Rule of Life as "[a] way of centering our commitment to a way of being and the rituals and practices that help us live our lives this way."

A Rule of Life is more than a treasured ritual or a value you live by. It's a way to declare the values that matter most to you, and rituals to help you live those values to the fullest. Maintaining these rituals is a powerful way to set boundaries that will help you define and uphold them in other areas of your life. They will also give you something to look forward to when you're in a stressful period or in the middle of a big project. Many of Kamala's values are outlined throughout this book you're reading, as are the rituals and practices she does to live them to the fullest. Your Rule of Life is the "what" and the "why" you define for yourself on what you want to get out of this life. You can adopt rules that you've been exposed to in your own life and in beliefs, adopt ones you feel called to, and write your own. Ter Kuile recommends you write a rule for a specific goal in your life, and to set a deadline. Free write on that goal: actions, statements, beliefs, questions, desires. Ter Kuile recommends you share the list with someone you trust, both for feedback and support.

I found myself inspired by Kamala's morning workout, and adapted it for myself using the Rule of Life structure. Here's a look at my Rule of Life for movement:

I want to be energetic and strong.

I feel really good after a workout.

Movement doesn't have to be a production. I can do it throughout the day.

I love and miss dancing.

Yoga makes me feel centered.

Walks in the park are a great way to break up the day.

Can I start my day with a little bit of movement?

Is bed yoga a thing?

I will move for thirty minutes a day. The thirty minutes can be broken down into chunks.

School drop-offs or anything where I'm looking at my phone does not count as movement. Unless I'm streaming a workout video.

Move before I open the social media and email apps on my phone.

In order to show up as your strongest, bravest self, you have to take care of yourself. Eat well. Move. Connect with your loved ones. Do the things that make you happy. Make these a priority, and give them the same effort that you bring to your work and your North Star.

Kamala's Tuna Fish Salad Sandwich

(via Kamala Harris's Instagram account)

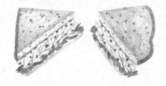

INGREDIENTS

1 can of tuna, packed in water

2 stalks of celery

2 tablespoons red onion, chopped

1 tablespoon mayonnaise

1 teaspoon Dijon mustard

Salt and pepper to taste

2 leaves of butter lettuce

Two slices of bread (Kamala uses multigrain bread)

Optional: parsley, lemon, cheddar cheese (should you want a tuna melt)

DIRECTIONS

Drain can of tuna, and mash it up with the back of a spoon.

Halve the celery lengthwise along the rib, and finely chop. Add the celery to the tuna.

Chop two tablespoons of red onion, following Kamala's hack below.

Add chopped red onion, mayonnaise, mustard, and salt and pepper to the tuna, and mix well. Add parsley and lemon juice to taste, if preferred.

Toast the bread and top it with the tuna salad mixture and lettuce.

For a tuna melt, spread mayonnaise on one side of the bread. Place the mayonnaise side down on the skillet, over medium heat. Add the tuna salad and top with sliced cheddar. Bring the heat to low, and cover until the cheese is melted.

How to chop an onion, KDH style

Chop an onion in half and remove the papery outer layers. Place one half on the cutting board, cut-side-up, and hold firmly.

Make shallow cuts on the open side of the onion, in
a crisscross pattern.

Place the onion on the side, and chop once.
Repeat as needed.

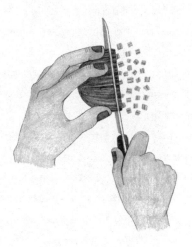

TAKING CARE OF YOURSELF — BECAUSE ONLY YOU CAN

by Naj Austin

I'm a Black, female, early-stage startup founder building a technology company funded by Silicon Valley firms—I'm familiar with rejection and the word *no*. As someone who has been in the industry for a few years, there are two things I've learned to be true when creating something the world has never seen. There's magic in seeing a vision grow into a realized product that exists outside of you. Alongside that joy there is a less-spoken-about energy centered around rejection and failure. There are people who don't believe in you, your product, or your vision, but still, we, as builders, must breathe life into our ideas. My company is designed around community, intention, and wellness — all qualities I lean on to help move through rejection.

I sit with the feeling. I don't give the feeling any more energy than it seeks but I experience and recognize it for what it is. Can this be a learning experience or a moment that will lead to inspiration? There is often a notion that one must seek vengeance or "spite build" — I think of it as an opportunity to get reinvigorated. I revitalize my vision and the product I'm building while seeking inspiration from things around me.

There is power in establishing boundaries — create them. This one is important because the lines can often blur between founders and their businesses. Rejection can feel personal and as a Black female founder there is often a pressure of building for a community that I feel I'm letting down. These boundaries can look like a reminder that you are not your work. They can look like taking a moment to journal, meditate, or phone a friend to remind yourself that you are you, not a rejection, and that matters most at the end of the day.

Find your people. There is both power and safety in a shared, collective experience. When dealing with any negative moments like rejection, I feel much better connecting with others in a way that feels authentic and nonperformative. I set thoughtful practices around who is on my care team for when days are rough: my small group of founder friends allow me to have a genuine space where I can unburden myself.

All of this can be summarized as "going through and not around it," which is a ritual I use in many ways throughout my life. You can't be your best self until you've created ways to work through all the sticky parts of what it means to be alive. That means accepting that within the good, we must also live through the bad, and that's okay. Creating boundaries is a responsibility you have to yourself—how can you continue to build, live, and thrive? How do you take back the power from a rejection and move forward?

"We always show up excellent."
— Shyamala Gopalan Harris

CHAPTER 6

Own Your Voice and Style

When Kamala speaks, you can't help but listen and pay attention.

At a lecture at Spelman College in 2018, she offered every woman assembled a powerful reminder of their own power. "I want you to know that when you walk, you walk into every room, when you walk into any room, when you walk into every room you ever walk into; do not be burdened by someone else's assumptions of who you are. Do not be burdened by their perspectives or judgment, and do not let anyone ever tell you who you are."

When a child asked her what she would do to stop police violence against Black Americans after the George Floyd murder, she answered honestly. "First of all, I think it's very important, always, that we speak truth—even when it may make people uncomfortable to hear it, and we might be uncomfortable speaking it. Unless we speak truth, we cannot confront the realities, identify the problems there are, and seek to change them. The truth is racism in America is real. The truth is that Black people in America, in many, many examples, have been the subject of racism, discrimination, racial profiling in the criminal justice system. We need to speak that truth."

When a reporter asked about how she brines a turkey before a live interview, she fired off her methods for both a dry and wet brine. Her wet brine includes bay leaves, sugar, peppercorns, and even a slice of orange. Her dry brine is salt and pepper, thyme, rosemary, and butter that should be rubbed under the skin of the turkey 48 hours before cooking (though 24 hours would work as well). She bastes her turkey with butter and cheap white wine.

When you interrupt her, she has two words for you: "I'm speaking."

Kamala Harris's voice carries authority and warmth. She opts for short, impactful sentences in her speeches and interviews. She is not afraid to go on offense in debates or hearings, with carefully worded questions delivered rapid-fire. But when she meets children, she's quick to kneel to their eye level, smile widely, and ask them about themselves.

Kamala honed her communication chops in the courthouse of Alameda County as an assistant district attorney, though not without a few fumbles. In one of the early cases she tried, she struggled to keep the directions straight on the map she was using before a jury. A self-deprecating joke landed her in Judge Horner's chambers. "Don't you ever do that [joke] again. You figure it out. Figure it out." She figured it out quickly, delivering her closing arguments without notes and looking the jury straight in their eyes. She prepared relentlessly for the hundred-plus cases she had at any given time, interviewing witnesses and studying police reports. Kamala honed her quick, pointed questioning style in the courtrooms of Northern California.

More important, she cultivated a deep sense of empathy as she prepared victims of sexual assault to testify in court. The victims were often children and teens, and would have to endure cross-examination and the jurors' judgment on top of their own trauma. Kamala's speaking style is an iron hand in a velvet glove. She's tough and unrelenting when the occasion calls for it, warm and soothing when necessary.

However, there is one central tenet to everything Kamala Harris says: the truth. Her memoir is titled *The Truths We Hold,* and "we must speak truth" is a common refrain in her speeches. The truth is not a sound bite for Kamala. It's the soul of every word she speaks. "I choose to speak truth," she writes. "Even when it's uncomfortable. Even when it leaves people feeling uneasy. When you speak truth, people won't always walk away feeling good—and sometimes you won't feel so great about the reaction you receive. But at least all parties will walk away knowing it was an honest conversation." The truth matters. So do the words you choose when you speak or write. It's why Kamala mandated dignified terminology during her time in the justice system, rejecting the terms "teen prostitutes" and "revenge porn" for "sexually exploited youth" and "cyber exploitation," respectively. These phrases assigned the blame where it rightfully belonged and offered the victims some semblance of dignity.

Finding the right words is one thing. Delivering them is quite another.

Kamala does not mince words. Her sentences are short and to the point, yet she paints a powerful picture with them. In her writing, she takes care to explain the context first, whether it's about the maternal mortality rates in Black women or why she became a prosecutor. Most women in positions of power shy away from emotion, but it's one of Kamala's greatest tools. When she talks about the many lessons she learned from her mother, she goes soft for a second before delivering her mother's words with strength and love. After visiting the Otay Mesa Detention Center to meet with mothers separated from their children, her words met the outrage she felt. "Look at this place behind me. We imprisoned them!" she declared at a rally outside of it. Kamala treads the emotional line carefully to avoid sexist and racist tropes. You'll rarely see her angry or hear her scream, but you will feel her outrage, disappointment, courage, and joy in the words she delivers.

When you're speaking personally to Kamala Harris, you feel like the most important person in the room. She looks you directly in the eye, asks thoughtful questions, and does not rush the conversation. Mark Buell felt this firsthand when he met Kamala to discuss her campaign for district attorney of San Francisco. Moved by her energy, her record, and the way she spoke, he was one of her earliest supporters and became the chair of her finance committee. I felt the same way when I met Kamala in 2019, while she was campaigning for president. She asked questions about my kids and inquired if they loved the same South Indian dishes she did. When I told her how she'd been my mentor from afar for the past eight years (mentioning my worn little notebook of Kamala-isms), she immediately wrapped her arms around me in a hug.

Kamala has the same focus and engagement when she delivers a speech, whether it's a small room with five people in attendance or on stage with tens of thousands watching. Every word she says, every gesture she makes, and even where her gaze lands is purposeful. There is no better example of this than the 2019 Liberty and Justice Celebration. Each presidential candidate's supporters flocked to the Iowa Events Center with signs, marching and chanting for hours before the actual event (formerly known as the Jefferson Jackson Dinner). Kamala memorably danced into the venue with the Isiserettes Drill & Drum Corp. Later that evening, she strode onto the stage to Mary J. Blige's "Work That" and delivered one of the most powerful speeches I have ever heard.

"I believe that in 2020, justice is on the ballot.

"When, in America, there is a father who is holding down two jobs, trying to figure out how to get through the end of the month, and paying more taxes than the richest four hundred families in America, economic justice is on the ballot.

"When, in America, there is a mother who is in a parking lot of a hospital afraid to walk through the sliding glass doors to get into the emergency room with her child, because she knows if she walks through those sliding glass doors, she'll be out of pocket a $4,000 deductible, health care justice is on the ballot.

"When we are looking at teachers, who across America, and here in Iowa, are holding down two and three jobs to get through the end of the month, education justice is on the ballot.

"When all over America, there are women who are being attacked for their constitutional right to make decisions about their own bodies, reproductive justice is on the ballot.

"When children in America, regardless of who their parent voted for to be president, are afraid to go to school because they are afraid they may get shot, they are afraid there will be a gunman roaming the hallways of their school, justice for children is on the ballot.

"So it is time that we fight.

"And this is a fight that is about all of us."

This speech was emotional, novel, and memorable, the three qualities of an inspiring presentation, as outlined in *Talk Like TED* by Carmine Gallo, a book that teaches the nine secrets of a successful TED presentation. Kamala did not hold back her true feelings during this speech. You could hear her anger and frustration at the reality that so many Americans face, and her passion to fix them. She positioned justice at the heart of every major issue, expanding our previous definition into something much bigger. Her new definition of justice was unique and suited to our times. Her repetition of "justice is on the ballot" reminded you of exactly what was at stake in the 2020 presidential election. Repetition is a powerful tool to make something memorable, and this speech certainly was. You don't have to run for president or aspire to give a TED Talk to communicate memorably. To start, you just need passion.

Although it's my main day job, I am not particularly passionate about the pharmaceutical industry. I am, however, passionate about improving the medicines we already know to be safe and effective so we can expand the uses for them and improve healthcare outcomes. You may think the news is one of my passions, given that I curate a daily roundup called #5SmartReads. What I am passionate about is learning more about the world we live in and the policies that will affect all of us—and sharing what I've learned with everyone I know, which was the inspiration for the series and why I've brought on curators who have different perspectives and expertise whom I've enjoyed learning from. I am very passionate about books, and would talk your ear off about how romance is a genre that deserves far more respect and acclaim than it currently earns, and will scribble down a list of books you absolutely have to read.

If connecting passion with your work seems daunting, just focus on the seemingly random things in your life that light you up. Unpack why you are so passionate about it. For me, reading romance shows me a world centered on consent, respect, and pleasure that often is contrary to our reality. It celebrates ambitious, smart women who refuse to settle because that's what is expected of them. Reading romance opened up my worldview in unexpected ways. Katy Evans's *Mr. President* introduced me to Jonathan Haidt's *The Righteous Mind: Why Good People Are Divided by Politics and Religion* well before the 2016 presidential election. It wasn't until I read about Kimba's journey with perimenopause in Kennedy Ryan's *Queen Move* that I realized I could be going through the same thing. Romance is an incredibly diverse genre that embraces multiculturalism, which has helped me live both my Indian and American identities more fully and wholly at the same time.

I could easily deliver a passionate TED Talk on why romance novels will save the world. But for now, I'll examine the way I talk and write about the romance genre, and bring that same energy to my pharmaceutical work or into #5SmartReads. The medicines our company develops are positioned to help millions, without increasing healthcare costs. #5SmartReads has helped thousands of women hold their own in conversations centered around politics and the news, arming them with the facts from multiple sources and a strong point of view. These are the visions I keep coming back to when I can't possibly respond to one more email or read another depressing news story. I take a second to focus on these positives before writing a response or my commentary on an article. I sometimes have to repeat this visualization while editing it to make it as impactful as possible. Having a North Star—something we talked about in Chapter 4—can help to bolster this exercise and keep you focused on aligning your work with your values.

Preparing for a speech or presentation requires more effort than responding to an email, but all of mine start with this visualization. I think about how I want the audience to feel and what I want them to learn after I deliver my remarks. Whenever I create my first draft, I do it with pen and paper, with my computer and phone well out of reach. I don't attempt to include details or facts at this time (though I'll keep a second list of ones I want to include in the presentation). The goal of the first draft is to build the foundation on the emotions I want to convey. I scribble down phrases and words that capture how I feel, the stories I want to include, and the key points I want to make. I go through a number of pages to get to an outline that I'm happy with, at which point I hop over to the computer and start typing it out. If I get stuck on a specific section or slide, I go back to pen and paper, getting my thoughts out longhand in a version of Julia Cameron's morning pages from *The Artist's Way*. In the mess of my random thoughts and feelings, I usually find that magic sentence or story that I'd been searching for.

This is the exact process I followed in writing this book. Whenever I stepped away from the computer and let my hands scribble all over a legal pad, the words and stories and advice came spilling out in a way they never did when I was typing. I'm not alone in finding my magic on paper and pen; former president Barack Obama drafts his speeches and his books the same way.

Writing the speech or creating the presentation is only half the battle. Delivering it is another, and public speaking can be incredibly intimidating. Anjali Kumar knows this all too well. As a member of the senior management team at Warby Parker, she was used to covering for the founders when they couldn't attend an event. They asked her to jump in for them at a TEDx event, where she learned that she would actually be speaking, not just attending. Cindy Gallop, advertising powerhouse and entrepreneur, offered Anjali the simple advice that she's carried with every speech: know your basic points, and tell a story. Anjali did just that, crafting an outline and selecting stories that emphasized each point. The success of that speech led to other speaking opportunities, both on behalf of Warby Parker and for Anjali alone. Years later, she delivered "My Failed Mission to Find God—And What I Found Instead" on the stage of TEDWomen, and this talk has been viewed more than three million times.

Delivering a speech—whether it's for one person or one million people—is intimidating. But Anjali implores you to remember two things. "One thing that was life changing is that everyone's rooting for you to win. The second is the cliche of 'people will forget what you said but not how you made them feel.'" Take a deep breath and step into the room knowing that people are hoping for you to succeed. Use stories to convey the points you want to make. Move about the space and make eye contact. Smile. Be expressive. Know that you are exactly in the place where you belong, and share your words with pride and joy and power. And if you are still feeling overwhelmed and nervous, take a page from Chapter 1 and borrow confidence. Take a deep breath. Push your chin up and your shoulders down. Smile. Speak.

YOUR STYLE

How you sound on a stage is one thing, but how you look matters, too. Kamala Harris's voice is powerful. So are her outfits.

Kamala's tailored suits are the armor she's donned since joining Alameda County as a prosecutor. While she's since swapped pencil skirts for straight-legged pants, the overall outfit has remained the same.

She typically opts for suits in tasteful neutrals. She stands tall in pointed-toe heels, adding height to her five-two frame. Kamala off-duty or on the campaign trail also dons a separate uniform: jeans, button-downs, and Chucks. No matter what she wears, you'll find pearls draped around her neck or in her ears, and gold bangles on her right wrist.

Despite this uniform approach to dressing, every item she wears is laden with meaning. Her first pearls

were a gift from her mother's mentor, and their significance only grew when she pledged Alpha Kappa Alpha at Howard. AKA's founders are often referred to as the Twenty Pearls, and every new sister receives a badge studded with twenty pearls upon initiation. Her collection of pearls ranges from classic strands and studs to pearls accented with gold details or strung on textured chains. On Inauguration Day, she wore a bold necklace featuring pearls suspended inside gold links and set with a diamond. Designer Wilfredo Rosado wanted to create a piece that was uniquely Kamala. "Kamala represents power and a tough woman and pearls are so gentle, feminine, and precious. When I think of hip-hop style, the artists are always wearing heavy chain links, and I decided to combine that with pearls," he said about the necklace. The gold chain was not just a nod to her Black American roots, but also to her Indian heritage. Hindu women often wear solid gold jewelry as a symbol of good health, power, and purity. Pieces crafted from 22-karat yellow gold are commonly worn by South Indian women, including Shyamala throughout her life. Gold bangles are traditionally passed down from mother to daughter, and Kamala wears hers on her right wrist. Her pearls and gold bangles are more than simple accessories—they are intentional choices to show the world who she is and where she comes from.

The rest of Kamala's fashion choices are just as deliberate. At Howard, students dressed for the jobs they sought to fill. Turtlenecks, blazers, and pearls were her trademark college style. Jill Lewis, her college friend and AKA sister, recalls, "You would find people on campus dressing accordingly [for the jobs they sought] and in Kamala's case, be carrying a briefcase around campus." Skirt suits with sheer black hose became her uniform when she interned at the Alameda County district attorney's office, and she kept wearing them as she was sworn in as a deputy district attorney until women were finally permitted to wear trousers in the courtroom. The collared blouses she wore early in her career were slowly replaced by crewneck tops in white or black, pussy bow blouses, or silk shells in the same inky blue, rich chocolate, or deep charcoal of her suits. Her professional footwear—pointed-toe heels ranging from three- to four-inch heights—have been a staple from the early days in her career. Kamala is rarely seen carrying a purse, but a few recent pictures show that she's swapped her briefcase for a large leather tote, filled to the brim.

Kamala's casual outfits are as basic as her professional attire. She wore her usual form-fitting jeans, a crisp crewneck tee, a blazer or jacket, and her beloved Chuck Taylors on marathon campaign days during her own presidential run and when she formally joined Joe Biden on the ticket. Her deplaning videos quickly went viral on social media, not for the outfits themselves, but how she wore them.

Despite opting for classic outfits most of the time, Kamala fully understands the power of fashion. While most of her outfits are formulaic, the specific pieces are selected with care based on how she wants to project herself. In the first Democratic primary debate, her CNN town hall, and in the 2020 vice presidential debate, she opted for a dark suit, a coordinating silk shell, pointed-toe heels, and her pearls. The outfits conveyed a bland gravitas we've come to expect from male politicians' outfits, focusing the attention on her words and not her attire. In later Democratic primary debates, her clothes made more of a statement in an effort to grab attention on the crowded stage—a royal blue suit paired with a white shell for a CNN–*New York Times* debate, a subtly patterned gray suit with a burgundy pussy bow blouse for the NBC News–*Washington Post* one.

When Kamala wants to stand out, she wields fashion to make it so. While the other women leaders wore suffragette white to deliver their speeches at the Democratic National Convention, she opted for a plum Altuzarra suit, a nod to the lesser-known color of the cause that signifies loyalty. She reserved white for her acceptance speech as vice president–elect, wearing a glowing white Carolina Herrera suit and silk blouse. After she suspended her presidential campaign, she returned to the Senate for a Judiciary Committee hearing with Attorney General Bill Barr. As it was her first public appearance and knowing that her questioning would be widely reported and meme-ified, Kamala donned a pink blazer with a black turtleneck and leaned into the press attention. One of my favorite fashion moments was the Levi's denim jacket adorned with crystals in a rainbow pattern that she wore with white jeans and pulled-back hair for San Francisco's Pride Parade in 2019.

Kamala's hair and makeup is the most consistent feature in her style over the years. Her hair frames her face in a sleek blowout with a bit of volume. Her makeup is minimal, but some extra eyeliner and mascara accentuates her eyes. She replaced the bright lipstick she wore at Howard with nude lipstick and a dab of gloss, drawing focus to the words she's speaking and the way she

delivers them. Ama Kwarteng reported on the vice presidential debate, observing that "Harris walks a fine line,
but she's able to visually appeal to so many different
groups at once, thanks to the softly bent hair, the glowy
and natural-looking makeup, the pearl earrings (and in
the past, colorful Converse and Timberlands). She's the
girl next door, no matter what neighborhood you live
in. And last night, she was able to nudge away any ideas
voters might have about female politicians being too
'aggressive' or too 'ambitious' with her style."

Beauty and fashion is one of the areas where
women—Black women in particular—must think
about and work twice as hard to be taken half as
seriously, and Harris's choices are proof of that. "We
always show up excellent," was one of her mother's
adages, and Kamala has lived up to it in her decades in
public life. Her style is classic and consistent, but it's also
true to herself. "I think there's real power in devising a
signature look because it's something that people can
expect from you. It helps craft a very reliable visual
brand," said Elizabeth Holmes, author of *HRH: So
Many Thoughts on Royal Style.* "When your style is
known for something, it's a way that people can support
and celebrate you. It's the way people close their eyes
and picture you. And I think it's very powerful."

Holmes's observation is astute, considering how many girls and women posted pictures wearing their pearls, blazers, and Converse for the inauguration ceremony in Kamala's honor.

Kamala's inauguration styles remained consistent with her classic style, but every outfit also had a deeper meaning to it. Nearly every item she wore was designed by emerging Black and South Asian designers. She opted for dresses for the majority of events, calling attention to her being the first woman elected to the vice presidency. The tan coat she wore to the COVID Memorial evening was designed by Kerby Jean-Raymond for Pyer Moss and featured a sculptured wave and long pleats in the back, marking a new wave of history for the country. Christopher John Rogers designed the rich purple coat and dress she wore for the inauguration ceremony. The bold color was selected to signify unity, the theme of the inaugural address and programming. For the Celebrating America concert, Kamala dressed in head-to-toe black, and the satin collar and liquid sequins of the Sergio Rossi outfit were intentional. "We kept the silhouette very structured and tailored, because that's who the vice president is. But the liquid sequins give her glamour and shine, because her influence and the way she's broken barriers is a light for so many of us. She shines so we can all shine," Rossi told *Town & Country*. Harris rounded out the inauguration events with a berry dress and jacket designed by Prabal Gurung (a Nepalese American designer who spent part of his childhood and early career in India) for the Inauguration Prayer Service. The color complemented her inaugural ceremony outfit, but also the seriousness of the event.

Personal style is just that—personal. But how you feel is how you show up to the world, and you deserve to feel your very best every single day. Kamala relies on her tailored suits, silky coordinating shells, and classic separates to bring her full self to work every day. These are her power pieces, a concept I explored in my first book, *How to Pack: Travel Smart for Any Trip*. Power pieces are the clothes you reach for time and time again that always make you feel like the best version of yourself. Scroll through your phone's camera roll and take a look at the pictures of your mirror selfies, and the pictures where you look and felt the happiest. What were you wearing? How did the clothes make you feel? Why did they make you feel that way? Consider the colors, the fabrics, and the cut of these clothes. It helps to keep your power pieces grouped together in your closet, so you can easily reach for them and study them to discover why they make you feel your best.

I have a few power piece outfits, each of them completely different from the other. When I have a big pitch or important meeting, I slip on a sharply tailored dress, a contrasting blazer or matching draped trench, my trusty three-inch black heels, and a structured leather bag. For marathon meeting days (both Zoom and in-person), I dip into my collection of wide-legged pants and matching tops, French-tucking the top into the trousers. A low-heeled bootie or velvet smoking slippers in the same color of the outfit finishes that power piece look. When I'm yearning for comfort and femininity, I reach for one of my caftans in bold colors and patterns, throwing on an embellished headband and furry slides to finish the look. Each of these outfits makes me feel confident and true to myself. I stand taller in these outfits and speak with greater conviction and clarity. While I still reach for my leggings and sweatshirts (especially in the mornings for school drop-offs and to incentivize myself to work out), I feel more focused, confident, and more *me* when I'm wearing my power pieces. And that's the energy I want to bring to everything I do.

Your power pieces might be a suit or simple separates

like Kamala's, or they might be something totally different. The most important thing to consider is how *you* feel wearing it. Does it make you feel strong? Beautiful? Powerful? Bold? Ready to tackle whatever may come? Does it meet the dress code for the occasion? Have fun with finding your power pieces! Think about your favorite characters on television or in movies, and put together similar ensembles from your own wardrobe. Play some music, try on the outfits, and see how you feel. Some might feel like a costume, and others might feel underwhelming or uncomfortable. If an outfit feels good, tweak it until it feels powerful. Does a different neckline make a difference, or do you stand a little taller in a certain pair of shoes (that you can also stand and walk in for hours comfortably)? Your power pieces should make you feel powerful, but they should also be comfortable. Don't be afraid to take some pieces to a tailor and have them tweaked to fit you perfectly.

Speak boldly and dress powerfully. What you say and how you say it matters. And whether we like it or not, how you look when you deliver it matters just as much. Choose your words with care. Deliver them with conviction. The audience will listen. Wear what makes you feel your most powerful. And if all else fails, a blazer and a string of pearls will suit just about any occasion.

YOUR STYLE IS YOUR POWER

by Rakia Reynolds

Black women have been using style to demonstrate their power for thousands of years. In ancient Egypt, women made bold statements by using makeup and jewelry to showcase their positions in society. The relationship between fashion and Black people is historically complex. We had to dress according to standards dictated to us by others, careful to fill the room with more than our skin color as a way to challenge the preconceived notions of who we were and what we were capable of accomplishing.

As a Black woman who has founded and runs her own successful multimedia communications agency with clients from coast to coast to coast, I am a fan of showing up to show out. Showing up means more than just occupying space, though—it's about doing those things that make you feel great and, subsequently, look good.

Work on yourself. Showing up in your full power takes work. Many of us still battle imposter syndrome and compare ourselves to someone else based on looks. Affirmations, morning meditations, and a mindfulness practice helps me realign daily, but my journey goes even deeper. I have spent years in thoughtful introspection, studying racism on a micro and macro level. The more I unearthed how racist ideologies show up in practice in my daily life, the more I was able to show up and show out, unbothered by the words and actions of others. This translates to everything from how I wear my hair and the color of my nails to the shoes I rock on red carpets and in meetings. This work is not easy or quick, but it frees you from the expectations of others that you have internalized.

Develop your signature style. I'm a natural storyteller, and that extends to my personal style. I dye my hair blue because I'm the face of my company, Skai Blue Media. I use earrings to help tell my story. For the first three years of my business, I wore octopus earrings to symbolize the entrepreneurial journey of having to do it all. Now I wear an eye earring that reflects this new season of my life, where I rely on my strong power of discernment to recognize the truths that surround me. My power is walking into a room and filling up the chair, and what I choose to wear helps me — sometimes it's a blazer with a fun sweatshirt that I've belted and paired with great boots. For more formal attire, I'll don a vintage suit with a tube top or bandeau underneath, the ensemble I wore to a tech conference in Toronto, where there was $3 billion worth of business in the room.

My style is a reflection of where I've been, who I am, and where I'm going, and I don't take that lightly. It's an opportunity to tell my story every day, in every way, so why should I make myself small in the story of my life? I choose to show up and show out. How will you step into the room tomorrow morning and flex your stuff?

"Family means everything to me. I've had many titles throughout my career, but Momala will always be the one that means the most to me."

CHAPTER 7

Lean on Your Family

CHOOSING YOUR FAMILY

Kamala Harris is many firsts. But her very first first is as the eldest daughter of Shyamala Gopalan Harris. Shyamala was an extraordinary woman. She defied expectations her entire life: immigrating to the United States to study science, marrying for love and subsequently divorcing her daughters' father, raising her daughters and granddaughter to be formidable women in their own right, and making groundbreaking discoveries in breast cancer research. Everything she did—from cooking dinner to running a lab—was performed with excellence and compassion. She was a grounding presence in her daughters' lives, from volunteering as class mom to attending every rally and campaign event she could.

Shyamala had two goals in her life: to raise her daughters and to end breast cancer. Every minute she lived, every decision she made, and every word she spoke was in service of those two goals. Her daughters were not the only ones showered with Shyamala's love and discipline. Shyamala offered this tough love to the graduate students that came through her lab, her daughters' friends, and even Kamala's first volunteers.

Shyamala rejected the false narrative that mothers are meant to do it all. She knew that she could not mother her children and cure breast cancer at the same time. When she was in the lab, she was laser focused on work. Her tight-knit community in Oakland all helped raise the girls, giving them precious memories and so much love from so many people. Mrs. Shelton's sunny day care was where the girls spent their afternoons after school. On Sundays, Mrs. Shelton collected the girls and brought them to church with her. Kamala made her way to Mrs. Jones's home up the street three times a week for piano lessons, and would visit Uncle Sherman to play chess other nights. Kamala recalls her mother bringing home flowers for the babysitter when she had a breakthrough at the lab, thanking them and telling them that she couldn't have achieved it without the sitter.

Having built a life away from her parents and siblings, Shyamala built a chosen family in her new home. Kamala and Maya benefited from the love and support from their chosen aunts and uncles, and built similar chosen families for themselves. Kamala learned early how to build her chosen family, in her early days at elementary school. Kamala has a tiny scar on her forehead. It came from a rock that a boy threw at her in kindergarten, when she intervened on Stacey Johnson-Batiste's behalf. The boy had grabbed Stacey's clay project and thrown it on the ground, where it shattered. Kamala defended her friend, and ended up with that scar. "The person people see and hear is the same person I've known since we were five years old," Johnson-Batiste told Bay News 9.

Kamala is the kind of friend we all hope to find and be. She treasures her friendships, many of them decades long. She remembers your birthday and anniversary, and will text and call you regularly to check in. Her loyalty is unflappable, and she will drop everything for you in the worst moments of your life. Her jokes and infectious laugh will have you in stitches as well. It doesn't matter how you met Kamala, whether it was on the bus to school, at university, if you were her opponent in the district attorney's race, while negotiating a settlement for the foreclosure crisis, or if your ex-husband was now married to her. Once you became Kamala's friend, you became family.

On the outside, these relationships appear effortless and natural, but every relationship worth having takes work. Another person who makes relationship-building look effortless is Susan McPherson, the founder of McPherson Strategies. The first question Susan will ask you is "How can I help you?" It's a question we don't hear too much lately, and one that might make us feel uncomfortable or slightly defensive. Our natural inclination is to dismiss the question and say "I'm good, but thank you for offering." But the truth is that we all could use help in something happening in our lives, and we can also offer help to someone else. In reflecting on the Harris family (the members born into the family and the chosen members of the family), help is the fiber that binds them together. And it goes beyond babysitting or sharing meals. Help can be offered in mentorship, something all the Harris women prioritize in their careers, as I'll share later. It can be loaning a friend a book that you adored and know they may, as well. It's sending a text the moment you wonder how someone is doing, or leaving them a voice memo asking how they are and sharing that you miss them.

These small actions are meaningful in maintaining current relationships, but what about building new ones? McPherson's "gather, ask, do" method that she outlines in her book *The Lost Art of Connecting* offers a blueprint to help us build new relationships. The way she practices "gathering" is to host an event, usually on the rooftop of her Brooklyn apartment building. "Ask" may sound self-serving, but McPherson's approach is quite the opposite. She asks if you have a trip coming up, or what would help ease a challenge you're currently facing, or simply "Is there anything I can do to be helpful to you?" Whatever you share in that conversation, you can expect her to follow up with an introduction to someone, an article you haven't come across that's tailored to your situation, or a list of recommendations to your next destination. The "do" step is what propels a conversation into a relationship, and repeating this process strengthens casual acquaintances into dear friendships—and into chosen family members.

Having these touchpoints to stay connected to your family members comes in handy when that family includes many nieces, nephews, and godchildren like Kamala's does.

EMBRACING AUNTHOOD

Kamala Harris's law school experience was slightly different than most of her peers'. Her days were spent in lecture halls, leading the Black Law Students Association and studying, as theirs were. But at home, she was in the throes of aunthood, helping care for her young niece Meena. "I'm dealing with this brutal stuff, dog-eat-dog in school," Kamala told Politico in 2018. "And then I would come home and we would all stand by the toilet and wave bye to a piece of shit." Shyamala and Kamala helped raise Meena as Maya completed her studies at the University of California in Berkeley and Stanford Law School. Meena speaks reverently about her childhood, likening it to the opening scene of *Wonder Woman*, where women led and ran a functioning society and saved the world. "I grew up surrounded by these strong, brilliant women who showed me what it meant to show up in the world with purpose and intention. My grandma was a single mom, my mom was a single mom, and then Kamala didn't have kids of her own when I was young. I just idolized them—these incredible women who were all around me," Meena told *Glamour*. "Seeing [them] and hearing [their] stories was formative for me."

Like her mother and aunt before her, Meena was a young participant in rallies and marches. She accompanied her mother to classes and meetings as a young child, just like her mother and aunt had accompanied their mom to rallies and to help out in her lab on weekends. The Harris women were raised to know they could achieve anything; excellence and service was expected. "You don't cut corners, ever," Kamala would tell Meena. "You always put in the work, and it's going to be hard work and oftentimes it'll feel like an uphill battle, but you put in the work."

Kamala has high expectations of the children in her life, but it's clear that they also bring her incredible joy. Her great-niece Amara was in her arms at the Oakland rally when she announced her run for president, and held her hand while walking down Pennsylvania Avenue in the inaugural parade. Meena shared a conversation between the two on her Instagram, with Kamala telling her great-niece that she could be president once she turned thirty-five, and Amara replying that she planned to be an astronaut president. "This conversation went on for like an hour," captioned Meena.

Kamala's godchildren are as precious to her as her grand-nieces, Amara and Leela. On election night in 2016, she comforted her young godson Alexander as she and her family awaited the results of her senatorial race, and as Trump's victory was becoming clear. As tears welled in his eyes, Kamala took him outside to comfort him, telling Alexander, superheroes "fight back with emotion, because all the best superheroes have big emotions just like you." Chrisette Hudlin named Kamala the godmother to her daughter Helena. "Kamala is so involved. She knows the teachers, she comes to every school play. They have sleepovers. She even took her on the campaign trail and they went all over the place — San Diego, San Francisco, Santa Rosa!" Hudlin told *Essence* in 2016. Kamala is also godmother to Micah and Kristopher Ernst, the children of her college friend Karen Gibbs. Micah recalls the closeness and normalcy of her relationship with her aunt Kamala throughout her childhood. Micah followed in her parents' and Kamala's footsteps by attending Howard, inspired and entertained by their stories from their college days. During the inaugural festivities, Kamala carved out time to see Micah and her parents, remarking at how proud *she* was to call them her family and express how important they are to her.

Kamala lights up whenever kids are around. At rallies, she would kneel down to their level and look them straight in the eye while having a conversation with them. When she was interviewed by child reporters during the 2020 presidential campaign, Kamala answered their questions clearly and honestly, and asked thoughtful questions in response. Children were always welcome in her campaign offices, and pitched in under Shyamala's wing. Lili was the nine-year-old daughter of Lauren Talmus, Kamala's fundraiser for the district attorney's race. Lili was a precocious, joyful child who also had Apert syndrome, which caused her head and face to be misshapen. Kamala always made time to speak with Lili when she saw her in the office, making direct eye contact and asking her how her day was going, how school was. "She just beamed in Kamala's presence," Talmus recalled in *Kamala's Way*. When Lili passed away from a seizure six years later, Kamala rushed to Talmus and Ace Smith's home to sit shiva with them, and has never once missed calling them on birthdays or Mother's Day.

Kamala is not a biological mother, and she is deeply maternal. Together, those qualities challenge the societal norms that women are expected to want to be mothers, and to birth children by a certain age. The reality is that many women, either by choice or circumstance, do not have children and don't plan to. These women are also deeply devoted to the children in their lives, showering them with love and attention and support. Kamala helps shift the narrative away from the stereotypes toward the reality and joy of being a devoted aunt to her sister's and friends' children, and later as a stepmother.

Savvy Auntie was one of the first online communities that brought together PANKs (professional aunt no kids) at a time where more women were childless or child-free. One out of every five American women in her early forties has never had a child, a statistic that has held steady over the past ten years. What *has* changed in the past ten years is the conversation around not having children. Women are more comfortable sharing their stories about why they never chose to have children, and there are more communities online to celebrate and support aunthood. Rachel Cargle's Rich Auntie Supreme celebrates the woman "who has decided to pursue the journey of being child free by choice & in turn intentionally indulges in the richness of being a meaningful part of villages around her." The mission of this community is to redefine "rich," expanding its definition from financial wealth to abundance in rest, time, space, and spontaneity. The Rich Auntie Supreme Facebook group has more than a thousand members who share memes, stories, and ask for advice.

Melanie's website was a valued resource for me when I was fully immersed in aunthood in my early twenties. I lived very close to my cousin and his family, and treasured my opportunities to hang with my nephews every week. I jumped at the chance to pick the boys up from practice. I loved taking them out to dinner and spending the weekends with them on the rare occasion both parents were traveling. My older nephew shared book recommendations with me, and my younger one was eager to whip up something new in the kitchen or visit our favorite sushi restaurant for dinner. I value those memories and my relationship with them, which has now morphed into résumé editing and making introductions for potential jobs. I treasure being an aunt to my cousins' and friends' kids, and I'm certainly not alone.

Grace Atwood is a writer and podcast host who has been forthcoming on her decision to not have children. "If my sisters hadn't had kids or if I didn't have sisters, I might be in a different boat with wanting my own kids. Or I may not," she told me. She's heard all the rebuttals to why she should have kids ("You'd be such a great mom!"), and it has never swayed her decision. She focuses her energy on her niece and nephews instead. She stays connected with her nephews with regular

FaceTime dates and surprising them with activity sub-scription boxes. Grace has a standing date every week-end with her niece, where she sets up an art project to do together and indulges her in toys or items that are equally adorable and absurd.

When it comes to having children, your choices and circumstances are your own. I celebrate and share com-passion with you and your reality. Sharing love with the children in your life—your own or those of your loved ones—is one of the best gifts you can give. Tech-nology has made it easier to get face time with our loved ones. If your nieces or nephews live far away from you, set up a regular video call date to stay connected. Ask the kids to share their latest book or their favorite toy of the moment, and do the same from your end. Talk about what they're learning in school. Read a book over the call, and mail them the book when you hang up. If you're able to see your nieces and nephews in person, plan an activity that their parents would typ-ically avoid (and clean up once you're done). As they learn to read and write, send them letters and save the ones they send back in return. For birthdays and holi-days, indulge them in the toys their parents are unlikely to buy them. My sons' aunts delight in buying them the noisiest toys like drum sets, whistles, and brightly colored toys with flashing lights and headache-inducing volume. In true form, my older son knows exactly who gifted each toy to him and drags it out whenever he has a phone date with that aunt.

As these kids grow up, so will your relationship. Your time together will gradually shift from playing with action figures and reading picture books to sharing playlists and going to see movies together. They'll start asking more questions about your life, wanting more details than you previously shared. Their questions shift from straightforward and slightly nonsensical to thoughtful and detailed. You may be the person they confide in before talking to their parents. You'll watch them transform from energetic, spunky kids to thoughtful, nuanced young adults. You'll become their friend, and confide in them the things you shared with your own aunts and uncles before discussing it with your parents. When I asked my nephew about the time we spent together when he was young, he connected those experiences with his desire to become a scientist. "Whatever I asked to cook, we would attempt it. Scallops, silk pie, cannoli. When we couldn't figure out how to make something, you showed me how to research and come up with different options. So while our PVC cannoli molds weren't exactly a success, you showed me that it was okay to try something and it not work out, which is the scientific method in action. You were always my cool aunt who I was so excited to hang out with. You're still my cool aunt, but also my friend."

It's time we expand our definition of "maternal." If you have love to give, share it with the kids in your lives. It's a precious gift you'll give them, their parents, and yourself. As a stepmother and auntie, it's a joy Kamala knows firsthand.

FINDING THE STRENGTH TO SAY GOODBYE

Our relationship with our parents changes as we grow up, shifting from a needs-based dependence to something new and unique to each of us. For most of Kamala's life, through childhood and then as an adult, her mother was her constant rock. She was a key leader in her first campaign for district attorney, dropping Kamala off to meet with voters throughout the city and holding down the fort at campaign headquarters. Shyamala assigned tasks to volunteers, helped plan events, and sat front row for every rally and speech. Shyamala beamed with pride as she held Regina Shelton's Bible while Kamala was sworn in as district attorney of San Francisco. Four years later, it was Kamala who ferried her mother to doctor's appointments and chemotherapy treatments. She often sat with her in the infusion room, keeping her company and running out to pick up the croissants she loved from a nearby bakery. Kamala administered her mother's medicines, logging any adverse events, and was in constant contact with the doctors (and making sure they were in contact with one another). As her mother's health declined, Kamala mothered her mother. She prepared her favorite meals, dressed her in the softest clothes and warm hats, and stayed with her as Shyamala protested having a nurse to help care for her. Shyamala was in and out of the hospital as her condition grew worse, with Kamala by her side.

Kamala had just announced her candidacy for attorney general during Shyamala's last hospital stay. Despite her mother's weak state, Kamala couldn't hide the truth from her. "Mommy, these guys are saying they're going to kick my ass," recalled Kamala in her memoir. "My mother had been lying on her side. She rolled over, looked at me, and just unveiled the biggest smile. She knew who she raised. She knew her fighting spirit was alive and well inside me."

None of us knows what the future holds in store for us. We don't know how long we have with our parents, nor the quality of life they'll have as they age. While we all want them to live long and healthy as possible, the reality may be different. All we can do is love our parents and elders as best as we can, and savor every second we have with them. Now, this isn't to say that you have to uproot your life and move back in with them this very second. But you can see and hear them with the phone that's probably sitting right next to you. Call them regularly, no matter if you have news or not. Ask them to share the stories you probably forgot or never heard from them in the first place. Send them videos and pictures that will make them laugh. Mail them cards on their birthdays and anniversaries, and visit them when you safely can.

For as much as the pandemic upended all our lives, I will treasure the four months we spent at my parents' home for the rest of my days. Months later, the days have blurred into one another. But I clearly remember the evenings we spent sitting at the dining table after my sons were asleep, sharing a glass of wine and laughing over what my kids did or what I used to do at their age. I treasure my twice-daily walks with my father, talking about work and the news and what Rho was blabbering about earlier in the morning. The late-night talks with my mom, sitting on the couch with a cup of tea, brought me such comfort after a marathon day of remote schooling and my own work and keeping my toddler off the stairs. My parents are both in their seventies and in good health as I write this. But if this pandemic has taught us anything, it's how quickly things can change. Make the call. Plan the visit. When you're with your loved ones, give them your full attention. If you have a difficult relationship with your parents, then please ignore this advice. Not every relationship in our life is a healthy and loving one, and you need to protect your heart and yourself.

Shyamala continues to live on in Kamala and Maya, in Meena and Amara and Leela, and in every woman she mentored and advised. "And though I miss her every day, I carry her with me wherever I go," wrote Kamala in her memoir. "And there is no title or honor on earth I'll treasure more than to say I am Shyamala Gopalan Harris's daughter. That is the truth I hold dearest of all."

HOW TO GRIEVE

by Marisa Renee Lee

When you lose someone you love, you are forced to figure out how to live a new life: life without your person. You experience tremendous pain in the weeks, months, and years after your loss, and as you move forward with your life, you will be forced to learn how to hold grief and joy simultaneously. You will have to reckon with their absence through every single good (and bad) thing you experience in your life, forever.

I lost my mother the year before Vice President Harris lost hers. I know what it feels like to hold dueling emotions every time you have something to celebrate. It is hard, but not impossible. Every accomplishment, every life milestone is colored by their absence and reminds you of the person who "should" be there but isn't. In the thirteen years since my mother's death, I've learned a few things that help me balance the bitterness that comes with personal and professional achievement:

Hold Space for Feelings: Know that life's blessings may bring up complicated or sad feelings, so hold space for them. Figure out what it is you're feeling exactly, and give yourself permission to feel it. It is okay. There is nothing wrong with you. You are allowed to be sad and miss your person even, especially, when you're celebrating something amazing.

Bring Your Person: I have been deeply intentional about what it looks like to bring my mother along for my personal and professional achievements. She was included in my wedding and in my time in the Obama White House. I take the time to be thoughtful and intentional so I can include her in my life milestones in ways that feel authentic to me.

Do NOT Apologize: Don't apologize for your grief. There is no "getting over it." You lost someone you love, someone who matters to you, you don't have to get over it, so don't let anyone judge you if you are struggling to figure out how to manage your grief.

During her victory speech on November 7, 2020, Vice President–Elect Harris said, "And to the woman most responsible for my presence here today, my mother, Shyamala Gopalan Harris, who is always in our hearts. When she came here from India at the age of nineteen, she maybe didn't quite imagine this moment."

I cried because I've been there. I know what it looks like to build a career, to build a life, and to achieve great things without the person who would be the most proud of you. It isn't easy, but if you're able to hold space for your feelings, bring them along, and commit to owning your grief you can learn to hold your pain and their pride, simultaneously.

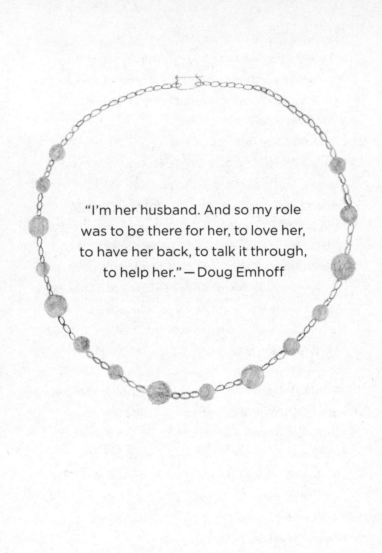

"I'm her husband. And so my role was to be there for her, to love her, to have her back, to talk it through, to help her." — Doug Emhoff

CHAPTER 8

Wait for Your Doug

Though her previous relationships caught the attention of the press, Kamala kept her romantic relationships close to her chest once she was elected district attorney. No one was the wiser, until a Los Angeles–based lawyer entered her life.

AIM FOR FAIRNESS

There are fewer things more attractive than a confident woman, and Doug Emhoff was immediately interested when a lunch meeting turned into an offer of a blind date with Kamala Harris. He had met Chrisette and Reginald Hudland for lunch to discuss a legal matter. At the end, Chrisette asked him outright if he was single, and said she wanted to introduce him to her longtime friend. She revealed the friend in mind was

Kamala Harris. "Oh, my god, she's hot," Emhoff recalls replying. Chrisette promptly started calling Kamala repeatedly, who finally excused herself from a meeting and went into the hallway to answer the call. "You're going on a date," she told Kamala. "He's cute and he's the managing partner of his law firm and I think you're really going to like him."

Kamala was hesitant, but she also knew there was no use in arguing with Chrisette. She asked what his name was. "His name is Doug Emhoff, but promise me you won't Google him. Don't overthink it. Just meet him. I already gave him your number. He's going to reach out." He sent her a text that evening, followed by a long, slightly rambling voicemail the next morning. She called him back during lunch, while she waited for her contractor to come by her apartment and collect the keys to start her kitchen renovation. The conversation flowed and both laughed freely for the next hour. Kamala flew down to Los Angeles for their first date, where Emhoff confessed that it felt like they had known each other forever.

The next morning, he wrote her an email. "I'm too old to play games or hide the ball. I really like you, and I want to see if we can make this work." The email continued with all his available dates for the next four months. After their third date—dinner in Sacramento, which he flew up for—they made the decision to commit to each other for the next six months, and reevaluate the relationship at the end of it. They continued to see each other when they could and spoke often, and Kamala met his children from his first marriage, Cole and Ella, a couple months later over seafood at the beach.

Doug made his debut as Kamala's significant other at the end of the six-month period, attending a speech on truancy she delivered at the California Endowment. Six months later, he proposed in her San Francisco apartment. They were married five months later in a ceremony officiated by her sister that incorporated their traditions. She placed a flower garland around his neck, and he stomped on a glass. Although they've been married for years, they are seemingly still in their honeymoon phase despite a Senate run, a suspended presidential campaign, quarantining together in their DC condo, and her election as vice president. "Doug and Kamala together are like almost vomit-inducingly cute and couppley," Cole Emhoff told *The New York Times*. "I'm like, When is this going to wear off?"

Finding *the one* feels impossible. Apps have redefined the dating landscape, distilling your whole self into a few pictures and pithy responses to random questions. We think we know exactly the kind of person we need, and sometimes reject people for superficial reasons. We date people for a time until we realize we're not on the same page about whether to have kids or where to live. Rejections are brutal, and breakups more so. We think we may have found a match, only to be dumped with little explanation. Love is very much a battlefield, and dating to find your long-term partner requires a lot of strength and self-care.

In my early twenties, my parents were eager to see me settled down with a husband, a common sentiment for South Asian parents who immigrated in *their* early twenties. My mother introduced me to the many sons and nephews of her tangential acquaintances, and even set up a profile on an Indian matrimonial site. I dated as well and had a lot of first dates, a few second ones, and only a handful of longer-term mini-relationships. I was happy being single, and was more focused on having fun than settling down. At twenty-five, my desire for a partner overtook my sense of fun. I asked the women in my life for their advice on how to date to eventually marry. My cousin's wife, Jessica, who is like a big sister to me, shared the advice that changed my life. "The men your parents keep introducing you to are settled.

They have their careers, their homes, and a very nice life. They're looking for a wife who'd be happy to fit right into the life they've built. You would be miserable in a marriage like that, which is why you never go on a second date with any of them." It was the first time someone had connected the dots of my dating life, my goals, and my parents' well-intentioned expectations for me. I asked her who I should be dating instead. "Look at the guys who are just getting started, like you are. You need someone you can build a life with, someone who shares your ambition and celebrates it. Look for the guy who makes you laugh so hard your stomach hurts, who appreciates the random things you're fascinated by. Someone who will challenge you, and teach you new things." Two months later, I met my husband at a networking conference. He had just started his MBA, appreciated my obscure *Gattaca* reference in one of our first conversations, and made it very clear that he was interested in a long-term relationship. And if I hadn't had that conversation with Jessica, there's a very real chance that I would have dismissed him immediately after meeting him.

There hasn't been a family quite like the Harris–Emhoff one in the public eye, but they represent the growing numbers of women in their forties without biological children, of men taking a career pause to support their spouses, and of blended and multicultural families in the United States. Kamala was in her late forties when she met and married her husband. She's a devoted "Momala" to Cole and Ella and is close friends with their mother, Kerstin. Doug took leave from his partnership at DLA Piper when his wife was named the vice-presidential nominee. Their story is a testament to staying true to yourself and not compromising your standards for a partner, in not playing the usual relationship games when you find someone special, and in making each other a priority.

Kamala and Doug entered their relationship knowing exactly who they each were, and what they each wanted to do. In choosing each other, they also chose each other's dreams and aspirations. "To me, the most important notion in twenty-first century couples is 'I see you now, and I'm going to do everything in my power to support who you want to become,'" observes Eve Rodsky, the author of *Fair Play*. Women in straight couples have traditionally been the ones supporting their partner's dreams. As second gentleman, Doug is showing the strength that comes with supporting your partner with joy and love. "My whole life has just been to support the people I love unequivocally, and they support me. The whole thing has been based on parity and mutual respect," Doug told *Marie Claire*.

Who you choose to commit to in a relationship is one of the most important decisions you'll make. Does your partner support who you want to become? Are you on the same page about some significant choices like children, pets, and lifestyle? Finances and how to manage them? Are you proud of each other's individual accomplishments? How do you tackle problems and challenges? Are you both fixed in "this is how things are and we have to operate within these confines," or do you push back and tackle challenges as an opportunity to change things? A growth mindset isn't just important in your career—it's even more important in your relationships. People change over time, and what's important to you in your twenties is so different than in your forties. This puts an intense pressure on you to pick the right partner, or to break up with someone who hasn't grown alongside you or doesn't share the same goals. And the only way to know these things about your partner and your relationship is to talk about them.

Strong relationships are rooted in strong communication. And it's not just talking about schedules or logistics or what to add to the grocery list (though we'll talk about those shortly). You need to check in with your partner regularly, to discuss your individual and mutual goals and aspirations, and how you can support each other in achieving them. Relationships are grounded in communication, but many of us lack structure around it, or making it a practice.

My husband and I have a weekly check-in on Saturday nights, where we review logistics and schedules and finances along with how each of us is feeling, and what we want to share with each other. These check-ins create a safe space for us to share the little things that we love about each other, but also annoy each of us. The pandemic certainly tested our relationship, doing away with our carefully planned schedules and throwing us into the whirlwind of work, remote schooling, a period of time with no childcare, and trying to make sense of it all. I took the lead on the schooling and childcare in the first half, taking calls while pushing my younger son in the stroller and letting my older one ride his scooter next to me, and catching up on work in the evenings. Five months later, my husband took a leave of absence from work and took on childcare and household responsibilities while I fully focused on running my company, writing this book, and taking better care of myself. In the chaotic days and late nights, we never lost sight of each other's goals as well as our own, and our weekly check-ins kept us connected to those goals. In spite of all this chaos, we each achieved some major milestones in our careers. My husband left consulting and became a venture capitalist, a longtime goal of his. I wrote this book that you're holding right now, executed a major partnership for our pharmaceutical company, and grew #5SmartReads.

On paper, it certainly seems like we have it all and everything is perfect. We have been born with privilege and have loving families that set us up for success. Our marriage fits neatly within society's expectations. My husband and I met and married in our mid-twenties and welcomed our two sons in our early thirties. We are privileged to own a home, and we each have careers that bring us a lot of fulfillment. That said, our marriage is successful because of the work and time we invest in it. And among all my accomplishments, my marriage and my family are some of the ones that I'm most proud of.

I suspect Kamala and Doug feel the same. Kamala lists "Wife and Momala" as the first two roles on her social media profiles, and "devoted dad and proud husband" are listed on Doug's.

CLAIM YOUR UNICORN SPACE

Kamala's warmth and empathy extends far outside her family and friends. Her onetime opponents have been the recipients of surprise calls or texts when mourning a recent death. Bill Fazio, who ran against her in her first district attorney's race, was surprised to get a call from Harris when his wife passed away, shortly after Kamala's mother had passed. "All she wanted to do was to talk about our personal losses in a very personal way," Fazio recounted to *The Guardian*. "People always call me up thinking I'm going to trash her. But I still feel really positive about her." Aaron Peskin, a member of San Francisco's Board of Supervisors, had been in the same class as Kamala from kindergarten to third grade. When Peskin's father passed away, he received a text from Kamala with a "thinking of you" message and a picture of the class book they had put together as kids.

Kamala is deeply devoted to the people in her life, and she holds them close to her chest. After the unwanted attention from her relationship with Willie Brown, she kept her love life extremely private while she was district attorney and attorney general. "As a single, professional woman in my forties, and very much in the public eye, dating wasn't easy," Kamala wrote in her memoir. "I knew that if I brought a man with me to an event, people would immediately start to speculate about our relationship." She attended these events alone, circulating the room with confidence and her joyful grin. It was far from easy, but it was the best option for her. "I also knew that single women in politics are viewed differently than single men. We don't get the same latitude when it comes to our social lives. I had no interest in inviting that kind of scrutiny unless I was close to sure I'd found 'the One'—which meant that for years, I kept my personal life compartmentalized from my career."

Many of us chafe at the expectations that society puts on us: to be married to a certain person by a certain age, have a certain number of children, live in a certain kind of home, and have a certain kind of job. One of the many things that is so inspiring about Kamala is how she rejects these stereotypical expectations and has always lived her life on her terms, much like her sister and her mother. Her career speaks for itself, but the same can be said for her personal life. From my perspective, Kamala prioritized her relationship with herself as much as she prioritized her career, and built a wonderful life that she loved living. The right partner would enhance her life, but she realized her dreams did not depend on who was at her side.

Your relationship with yourself is the most important one you'll have, but it's the one we often prioritize the least. We often put everyone else's expectations—those of our family, friends, bosses, and coworkers, even cultural expectations—ahead of our own before we stop to consider if this fits in with the lives we want for ourselves. When was the last time you spent more than thirty minutes doing exactly what you wanted to do? When was the last time you felt a sense of peace and flow in doing something just for yourself? There is a disproportionate burden on women, both at home and in the workplace. In the office, women (and especially women of color) are the ones tasked with office "housework," like ordering lunch for a meeting, pouring coffee for a client, or even closing the door of a conference room when a man is seated closer to the door. A study published by the Institute for Women's Policy Research, focused primarily on straight couples, found that at home, women spend two hours more each day on housework than men on average. While these numbers are glaring, the pandemic only made things worse, as mothers largely took on remote schooling duties while juggling work and keeping their households running.

There is no better time than now to shed expectations that no longer have a place in our society, and to boldly live the expectations you have for yourself. This starts with your "unicorn space," a concept coined by Eve Rodsky in her book *Fair Play*. Unicorn space is the "active pursuit of what makes you uniquely you." It's the time and space where you do the things that bring you joy, with no regard to productivity or expectations of others. When you're shouldering an unfairly heavy load at work and at home, unicorn space is all but impossible to come by. We also make a lot of excuses to not claim our unicorn space, citing our overflowing to-do lists and remarking at the little time we have for basics like eating or sleeping. We've been socialized to believe that having time to ourselves somehow makes us a bad partner or parent, that we're supposed to find joy in the overwhelming drudgery of housework, both in our workplace and in our homes. You have always had your own passions and interests, but they've probably been sidelined as time has gone by and life has grown busier.

The first step in claiming your unicorn space is to reject these narratives outright. Who you are is not defined by the home you live in, the partner in your life, or the children you may have. All of us spend hours doing the work we don't want to do. How much of that work is necessary, either for your household or for your happiness? Where can you make tradeoffs, either by offloading the task to someone else or doing away with it entirely? Are you able to adjust your budget to outsource some of these tasks? Make a list of all the things you're doing right now—at work and home, and even the little things you do that eat into your day, like checking email or Slack for new messages but not responding to any, scrolling social media, and browsing your favorite stores online.

Once you've filled this list, take a step back before you return. When you're a little more refreshed, examine the list and begin editing. Can you optimize meal prep by using a delivery kit for a few dinners? Does your budget allow for a robotic vacuum to help keep your floors dusted? Are you doing that workout because everyone else is, or because you actually enjoy it? Can a partner or roommate take on some of the tasks that you loathe but are absolutely necessary? Edit this list ruthlessly, delegating the items you can and editing others to free up more space and time in your life. This is a practice you'll want to revisit every six months or so, as things creep in and start claiming your unicorn space. Things change—your work, your family, your living situation, and you. This list should be as fluid as life is, so revisit it regularly or when you're adjusting to any big new change.

Once you have time and space, you can discover your unicorn space. Mine is reading and crafting. Most days, I carve out my unicorn space in the morning and the evenings. There's something about starting and ending the day on my own terms that is so transformational. My morning routine is focused on productivity and starting the day on the right foot, but my evenings are for what I *want* to do. In the evenings, once my kids are in bed and my husband is enjoying his own unicorn space, I work on my latest needlepoint project while listening to an audiobook. This ritual is incredibly relaxing, and seeing the progress I make every evening on my canvas is deeply satisfying. My unicorn space makes me feel like *me*. I've been an avid crafter and reader since I was young, so filling my unicorn space with these activities reconnects me to the person I've always been, now and into the future. I am a more patient mother, a more compassionate partner, a stronger leader, and a more self-assured person as a result of this time for myself. There is nothing more attractive than someone with a deep sense of self that they carry with confidence and pride. You deserve this. You've earned this.

Take some time to think about the things you loved doing as a kid, or the hobbies you've always wanted to do. Pick one of those things, and make a list of all the microsteps you can take toward accomplishing it. Have you wanted to read a certain book series? Step one is purchasing the first book in the series or taking it out from the library, and then putting time on your calendar to actually read it. If you're someone who craves community, text a few friends to join you and schedule a day to meet and discuss it. This is how I accidentally started a romance book club for a group of my close friends, many who traditionally read nonfiction. These gatherings help me stay accountable to my unicorn space, but also bring a deeper sense of joy and belonging when we get together to discuss it.

Unicorn space is the ultimate act of self-love. It's a practice that helps you shed the expectations placed on you and live your life on your terms. It positively impacts every area of your life. It gives you the confidence to show up in the world in all your power, rejecting the expectations of others.

The most important relationship is the one you'll

have with yourself. The one with your partner is a close second. In making both a priority, you will be able to endure the hard times and enjoy a honeymoon-like bliss in the good ones. And if you're very lucky, the honeymoon goes beyond the first months of marriage—just like Kamala and Doug.

THE POWER OF CHECKING IN

by Kat Cole

I was six months past ending an eleven-year relationship, with no intention or desire to meet the love of my life so quickly, but I did. Daley—who is now my husband—was also recently out of a long-term relationship. He and I met at an impact event and had a one-night stand (so we thought). Within weeks we were proposing marriage to each other.

As it became clear that we didn't want to be with anyone else, we reflected on what we had learned from past relationships, what we admired in any successful partnership, and agreed we wanted to be even better at home as partners than we were at work. This alignment of wanting to be a great partner first and foremost was new for both of us. It led to us asking, how do we care for this relationship proactively, from the beginning, and not be one of those couples who wait until there are issues to be intentional?

Daley recalled reading about a couple who had a monthly celebration of their love, and we loved the idea of celebrating our "monthiversary." We agreed that on the tenth of every month (the monthiversary of our meeting), we would protect time to celebrate each other—a coffee date, a dinner, a glass of wine—in person or virtual, no matter what. And while that felt great to commit to protecting a time, it wasn't enough to just "cheers to our love."

We discussed the best practices of leadership, teams, and high performance, and agreed that this monthiversary could be both a celebration and a moment of reflection and communication to help us grow as a couple. We drew on some of our professional training as leaders to come up with a series of questions that would allow us to check in on things affecting our relationship for the past month. These monthly check-ins were not to replace real-time communication, but rather to hold a space for the sole purpose of going deeper, tapping into highs and lows and actions we could take that lasted beyond any moment.

The questions in the check-in are about tapping into both the great and not-so-great, and, most important, identifying what we can do differently to be better for each other, little by little, month by month.

Quick Start Guide to Our Monthly Check-Ins

My husband and I want to show gratitude, honor our relationship, and intentionally grow. We reserve thirty to sixty minutes each month on our monthiversary for our check-in. We review the last thirty days via our calendars, because who remembers last week, much less all month? We then go through our questions.

The first six questions start with, "When you look back at the last thirty days, what is…"

…the best thing, event, moment, memory?

…the worst thing, event, moment, memory?

…one thing I can do differently (more, less, etc.) to be a more effective/better partner for you? (We used to ask for only one thing, but a few years in, we wanted to get more specific, so we changed it to listing one thing to stop, one to start, and one to continue.)

…your biggest worry?

… your biggest point of pride/brag?

… your greatest gratitude?

Optional share: What is the thing that I/we spent money on that provides the most/least value?

Goals check: How can we help each other with goals or interests? (Pick one or two, then ask for and offer help.)

Progress check: What is one thing I have improved and/or not improved from our check-ins or stated commitments and goals?

What is an area we want to improve or focus on with family/kids?

The goal is to dig deep, be specific and candid, listen and feel, ask clarifying questions, have more discussion if applicable, and grow for each other and ourselves. This *does not* take the place of discussing things in real time — it is simply checking in on what stands out most from the last thirty days.

Each quarter we do a deeper dive, which is sometimes a vacation weekend or a "staycation" day (which just means getting a babysitter for a few hours). We make time to go through past check-ins, personal and professional goals, family goals and progress, calendars for the next quarter, and make any updated commitments. We also do an annual check-in to wrap up the year and prepare for the next.

As we've shared this practice with friends and family, we have seen it evolve and make a positive impact in their lives. Never having missed a month since we met, I can say that these check-ins have become a foundation of our relationship and provided moments of celebration and deep connection.

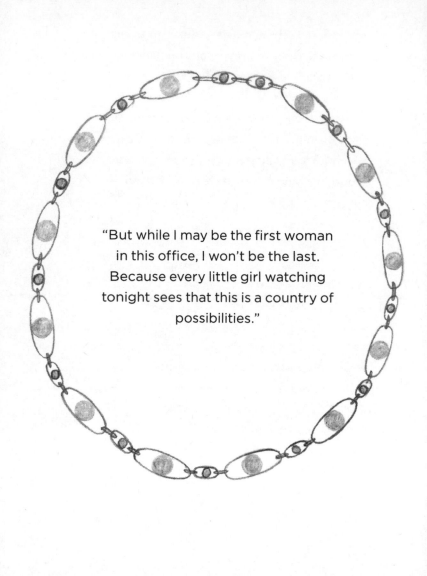

"But while I may be the first woman in this office, I won't be the last. Because every little girl watching tonight sees that this is a country of possibilities."

CHAPTER 9

Don't Be the Last

CHANGE THE FRAME

by Samira Panah Bakhtiar

I'm a tech executive who has earned executive roles at two of the largest technology companies in the world. I am also a New Yorker, a Millennial, a wife, daughter, sister, mother to two children under the age of four, and also happen to be a second-generation Iranian American born into a Muslim family. "Don't be the last" was not a phrase, but a North Star that was cultivated by my experiences.

My career began in 2006, in Cisco Systems' Sales Associates Program. In 2007, I was placed into a field assignment based in New York covering a large cable and media company. At that time, I was one of the only Millennials and women of color at Cisco within this division. I was surrounded by white men who were far more technical — many of whom had worked in cable and media longer than I had been alive. These gaps (generational, racial, and technical knowledge) triggered my imposter syndrome. I struggled to find commonality of culture, style, or cause, which drove me to assimilate out of a massive desire to feel accepted. I began to portray myself as older, whiter, and more masculine. The entire situation made me doubt myself, and this doubt and imposter syndrome in the early parts of my career grew as I moved up the ranks into leadership roles over the years.

As I took on management responsibilities, I shed the masculine, whitewashed persona I had donned and showed up as myself. The biggest lesson I have learned is to own my authenticity, realizing that I am enough. I don't like to be viewed as the sum of my parts, but the whole of my contributions. There are lots of different parts of me, and how all of them make me *me* is what matters most. And when I had to hire and build teams, I looked for people who brought the whole of their contributions to the table and who represented the world as it was, not the industry for what it had been.

This intersectionality played a critical role in both my personal and professional life, as it has 1) led me to be more empathetic and compassionate, and produced a fundamental perspective that I would not have developed otherwise, and 2) fueled my grit and ambition, which have driven my professional success.

Based off all this, here is what I would share with you:

Change the frame. The moment we stop trying to compare ourselves, the easier it will become for us to become grounded in the tasks we need to accomplish. So much of our energy and power is wasted trying to assimilate, or worse, worrying about what others think! We all need to embrace our individuality and realize that it is our merit that propels us.

Know the signs of imposter syndrome. I remind those I mentor of a few things when combating imposter syndrome: Remind yourself that you are not alone — when I acknowledge that three-fourths of my peers are feeling the same insecurity, it dissipates the stronghold effect of imposter syndrome. Similar to work in mindfulness, if you can name the emotion you are experiencing, it helps to reinforce that the feeling is fleeting.

Build the teams you always wished you could have been a part of. I think back to the twenty-three-year-old version of myself. I was totally shell-shocked by what it was like to be in tech at a time when diversity, equity, and inclusivity didn't exist. As I stepped into management roles, I was cognizant of building teams that looked like the world we live in, not just the way tech has always been. Each of us has the power to stand for one another and pave the way for the next.

Ultimately, the diversity of experience that this intersectionality has provided has underscored the importance of using my privilege, and the platform that has come from it, to pay it forward and build a better future for the next generation of females and underrepresented professionals. Each of us has the ability to move, lead, and inspire those around us. Let's ensure we are not the last.

It was two months to the day before the 2020 Iowa Caucus. Kamala Harris had evaluated every single option left to her, consulted with her team and family, and made one of the most difficult decisions in her life.

In a blog post shared on Medium, she wrote, "I am not perfect. But I will always speak with decency and moral clarity and treat all people with dignity and respect. I will lead with integrity. I will speak the truth...I've taken stock and looked at this from every angle, and over the last few days have come to one of the hardest decisions of my life. My campaign for president simply doesn't have the financial resources we need to continue."

Suspending her presidential campaign was one of the most difficult moments of Kamala's professional life. After a successful launch, her campaign struggled to raise money from individual donations and wealthy donors alike. Her position on certain issues wavered as the campaign went on, especially on Medicare for All. Her record as a prosecutor was dissected from the context required to understand the issue holistically, and her opponents seized on these misinterpretations and landed blows in the debate. Kamala's offensive debate blow to Joe Biden on busing was a short-term victory, but her polling numbers continued to fall into the single digits after. Like many campaigns, there was conflict within her own team. All of these are unfortunately the norm for most primary presidential campaigns, no matter the party. But Kamala faced challenges that few others ever had.

"The media—and voters—tends to set such a low bar for the Republican champion they send before the people to try and best the Democratic opponent, for whom there's such a high bar," wrote Tiffany Cross in her book *Say It Louder*. "The bar gets higher when it comes to Black candidates and becomes a nearly insurmountable hurdle when it comes to Black women." No other candidate faced questions on whether they were Black enough or were questioned about their support from Black voters, which, ironically, were posed by mostly white journalists. Glowing media coverage was largely reserved for the leading candidates: Vice President Joe Biden, Senators Bernie Sanders and Elizabeth Warren, and Mayor Pete Buttigieg. Coverage influences voters' perception of each candidate, and the reporting on Kamala was focused on her brief answer to a question about her smoking marijuana, posed on the Breakfast Club radio show, with no reporting on her lengthy commentary on the LIFT Act. Biden's stewardship of the 1994 Crime Bill and his treatment of Anita Hill was sanitized by favorable reporting of his overwhelming support among Black voters as Kamala's coverage focused on why she was struggling to get the support from her own community. "There's a willingness to forgive white people for doing something racist in their past... Newly woke white people were welcome to our votes, but a Black person who made a policy misstep should have foreseen the unintended consequences that would harm her brethren," Cross wrote in her book.

After her disappointing presidential campaign, Kamala redefined her narrative completely. She identified the weaknesses in her relationships with various communities, and reached out to strengthen them. She learned how to tell her story with greater ease, speaking about her multicultural upbringing with confidence and sincerity. She made public apologies for the consequences of actions taken while she was district attorney and attorney general of California. She opened up on Instagram Live videos, showing chef Tom Colicchio her method of chopping an onion while talking about the struggles restaurants and the food industry were facing in the pandemic.

Kamala also endorsed Joe Biden shortly after Senator Elizabeth Warren—the last woman in the primary race—suspended her campaign. As the primary whittled down to the last two candidates, Kamala's popularity began to rise once again. "Interestingly, by the time the field narrowed to all white men, there was a strange nostalgia for her and regret that she was no longer on the stage," Cross wrote. "Perhaps having the benefit of hindsight, voters would find her more palatable as Vice President."

When it came time for Joe Biden to select a running mate, he embarked on a lengthy process that evaluated a number of powerful women in the Democratic Party. The ideal candidate needed to be a strong debater, be able to help Biden win the general election, be ready to be president, and bring diversity to the ticket. Kamala had made strides of her own after dropping out of the presidential primary, building bridges with Black activists on racial justice issues and sponsoring important stimulus and racial justice legislation in the Senate. As the vetting process went on, Kamala reached out to Dr. Jill Biden and Valerie Biden Owens to make amends from her attack on Biden's position on busing from the first primary debate. Her longtime friendship with the late Beau Biden also smoothed the tensions between her and the Biden family.

"You're going to have to work twice as hard. Nothing's going to be handed to you," Shyamala told her daughters, over and over again. It's not enough to work hard and speak well. Overcoming the microaggressions—and some macro- ones—while excelling at your job and mentoring others is a burden they have borne for centuries. This is the double standard that people of color, especially Black women, live with every single day. Kamala Harris's success is even more remarkable when you consider she battled this standard in every role she's held as a prosecutor and in every election she has won. She, like so many women of color, earned her power not just through her work, but also in overcoming systemic obstacles that stood before her. In nearly every instance, she was successful. Her first presidential campaign is the only one she did not win outright, though she did emerge victorious as the vice presidential candidate alongside Joe Biden.

Kamala thrived within Biden's disciplined campaign, speaking to his platform with grace and intelligence and formidably debating Vice President Pence in the October run-up to the election. Videos of Kamala jogging down the airplane steps in her Chucks and blazers went viral, as did her dancing in the rain in a parking lot rally in Florida.

"Yes, sister, sometimes we may be the only one that looks like us walking in that room," she said at a rally in Fort Worth, reported by *The New York Times*. "But the thing we all know is we never walk in those rooms alone—we are all in that room together." In the many rooms Kamala entered as the only woman (and a woman of color, at that), she brought with her the many women who came before her. She stands on the shoulders of Mary Church Terrell and Mary McLeod Bethune, Fannie Lou Hamer and Diane Nash, Constance Baker Motley and Shirley Chisholm—the Black women who led the fight for a better America. She stands on the shoulders of her mother and grandmother, women who were born before their time and fought for women to live their truth and achieve their wildest dreams.

While the 2020 Democratic primary didn't unfold the way Kamala expected, the general election did break some glass ceilings. When the election was called for Biden–Harris on November 7, she made history as the first woman—and first Black American and South Asian—elected as vice president of the United States. The Biden–Harris ticket earned more votes than any campaign in American history, and also flipped two reliably Republican states in the process.

Despite everything you do, there will be times when things don't work out the way you planned. You'll fall short of your lifelong dream. Other people's perceptions of you will be obstacles you can't overcome, despite your best efforts. You'll fail to gain traction for a million different reasons, many of which you'll struggle to identify months and even years later. My best friend Samira and I started Bridge2Act, a tech startup that aimed to bridge digital publishers, vetted nonprofits, and people wanting to take action the moment they read or watched something. We worked tirelessly to bring leading nonprofits onto the platform. We pitched the platform to publishers and influencers constantly, jumping onto calls with them and helping them create donation links to drive impact. We launched celebrity-driven campaigns to scale and bring in new users. We built a strong platform that worked beautifully and helped drive tens of thousands of dollars in donations, but we struggled to get traction and scale in a meaningful way.

Winding down the company was heartbreaking and left me feeling incredibly low. Over time, I was able to identify the weaknesses in our business model and observe the challenges of the ecosystem and time that we were operating in. The experience left me scarred, but with a greater sense of understanding how to make money as a business, prioritizing the most value-added work, and how to manage a team. Building—and subsequently closing—Bridge2Act has made me a better operator of a business, as well as an adviser and investor in startups. In the moment, I felt like an utter failure and a fraud as an entrepreneur. I had defined myself by the company so much that I forgot who I was, and I had to get to know Hitha again.

It seems simple enough, but how do you relearn who you are? "I tell myself a new story about myself every day so I can meet the most authentic version of myself," said Minda Harts. On a personal level, it's incredibly impactful advice. And on a larger level, having Kamala Harris as our vice president reminds us to show our multitudes and our whole selves every day, even when things don't work out as planned. "I know we often say that representation matters and it sounds very cliche in many ways," Harts said. "I raise my head a little higher knowing that there's a woman that looks like me in the administration. Being able to see that while you're alive, working and building. I can see how working hard and building the right relationships and being true to yourself does pay off. Kamala is the evidence of what is possible, and it makes me work even harder and build a better country so that there will be others that can also be the evidence for our future generation."

You'll never know who will need to see you show up in your power and to be the first to do something. Showing up is the first step in not being the last.

BUILDING YOUR OWN TABLES

Lateefah Simon never expected to work in the district attorney's office. She had visited the Cole Street Youth Clinic for medical care as a teenager, and tried to steal condoms to pass around the locker room of her high school. When she was caught, the clinic gave her a box of condoms, which she passed out to her classmates and shared more information about the clinic. Simon became one of the clinic's first peer educators, teaching other young people about reproductive health and safe sex.

That job led to a position as a street outreach worker at the Center for Young Women's Development. Within three years, she was the executive director of the organization, taking over from the founder. Shortly after, she met a prosecutor in the city attorney's office. Simon joined Kamala Harris for "know your rights" sessions for young women throughout the city. When Kamala was elected district attorney, Simon was one of the first people she asked to join her office. "I never wanted to work for The Man," Simon told *Mother Jones*. "And she was like, 'You'd be working for this black woman.'" When Simon demurred, Harris made her case more plainly: "You can bring your advocacy into the office, but do you forever want to be on the stairs yelling and begging for people to support you, your cause? Why can't you fix it from the inside?"

Simon told Kamala that it would be a risk to hire a "teen mom with no college degree," (neglecting to mention that Simon had earned the prestigious Mac-Arthur Fellowship—also known as the "Genius Grant"—as the youngest woman ever to do so and the only one with a GED). Kamala won her over, and supported Simon to earn a college degree while she served as the director of reentry programs. She enrolled in Mills College, and Kamala would review her report cards every semester. Kamala was a strict boss. Her office was always tidy, calls and emails were responded to promptly, and she required the same from her team. When Simon arrived at a Back on Track training in jeans and a sweatshirt, Kamala pulled her aside. "Why would you ever disrespect your people? You work for this office. You work for the state, so you represent. Would you go to Pacific Heights [a wealthy neighborhood in San Francisco] wearing that?" Simon recalled to *Mother Jones*. Kamala later gave Simon a crash course in what she called "executive presence," and handed her a garment bag. Inside was a brand-new suit, one that still hangs in Simon's closet.

Kamala's mentorship wasn't limited to her team. She took care to build relationships and mentor other Black women seeking higher office in competitive races. She reached out to Lauren Underwood, a former nurse running for Congress in a predominantly white suburb of Chicago, as she was mounting her campaign. "There's not that many Black women who have been at the highest level of politics in this country. Not that many Black women who have run very competitive races," Underwood told *The New York Times*. "To have the opportunity to learn from, counsel from, and just know someone who has done that is something I find incredibly valuable."

Within twenty years, Kamala Harris went from being a prosecutor to becoming vice president of the United States. And in every instance where she was the first woman or woman of color to hold the role, she surrounded herself with other firsts as well, putting them in charge of her landmark programs and mentoring them with tough love. She held these women to the same high standard she holds herself, and they've in turn done the same as their careers have grown. Lateefah Simon is now the president of the Akonadi Foundation and was elected to serve on the BART Board of Directors in 2016, winning her reelection bid in 2020. Underwood won her race in 2018 and had three bills she sponsored signed into law in her first term. After winning a tight reelection race, she was named to the powerful House Appropriations Committee and introduced the Black Maternal Health Momnibus Act of 2020, addressing Black maternal health with a number of measures.

The core principle of this book is to identify the false choices and narratives we find ourselves confined in, and to reject them outright the way Kamala Harris has. The myth of the exceptional woman—that only one woman can hold the power and position that men traditionally hold—is one that Kamala has been rejecting her entire life. This myth has been carefully preserved in every power structure that exists in our society, in government, in business, in investing, in education. "It's a false dichotomy that you have to dim your light to make room for others, and part of how they try to silence us and create discord," Nathalie Molina Niño told me.

Not being the last means we reject this narrative entirely. Feminine power is rooted in community and a collective sharing of power. We know that the sum of our parts is stronger than the individual, on how to work together to solve problems from their root, to check our egos at the door in service of the common good. Not being the last is a conscious choice that can be practiced in a number of ways. If you're approached with an opportunity (a speaking engagement, an interview request, joining a committee), ask who the other participants are. Are you one of the only women speaking at this event? Are you the only person of color participating in a certain campaign? There's a good chance that you're one of the only women, or people of color, or "othered" in some way. If you are, respond with gratitude and some recommendations. If you're working on a project at work or are asked to join a committee, list a few people who would be a valuable addition to the group. If you've been asked to speak at a conference and you're one of the only women or people of color, respond graciously but firmly. "It is important to me that I lend my voice to events that prioritize diversity and inclusivity, and I do not see that reflected in the speaker roster. I would be happy to recommend some powerful voices to join me in speaking at your event."

After noticing how I was often the only creator of color to participate in many of my sponsored campaigns, I created an inclusion rider in my responses. I have a list of incredible content creators of color who I recommend join me in the campaign, or to participate instead of me. As you grow in your career and into your power, you will learn that you have nothing to lose in respectfully challenging the status quo. And the more each of us brings new voices and perspectives into the rooms where decisions are being made, the more firsts and fewer lasts we have.

Not being the last is putting together the lessons from every chapter from this book. It starts with rejecting the expectations and narratives people attempt to assign to you and showing up with pride in your name and your multitudes. It requires a tireless work ethic and to bounce back from rejections. Ambition will fuel you, and showing how you've grown will increase your base of support. A clear North Star will keep you focused, and resilience will keep you strong when you face challenges. You'll learn how to overcome rejections and false choices while taking care of your body and your soul. Your voice and your style will tell the world exactly who you are. Your family and friends will support you every step of the way. You will overcome the obstacles that are too often placed in our way by virtue of your gender and race, and you'll come back stronger when things don't go as planned. You won't do this alone; the people you bring into your fold as you rise will rise as well, and do the same for others.

In her first speech as vice president–elect, Kamala said, "Dream with ambition. Lead with conviction. And see yourselves in a way others may not, simply because they've never seen it before." You were born to fulfill your ancestors' wildest dreams. You are here to challenge the way things are and help build a world on how they should be. You are strong. You are relentless. You are joyful. You are passionate. You will change the world. And you won't be the last to do so.

You are speaking.

Acknowledgments

They say to never meet your heroes. But meeting Vice President Kamala Harris on a rainy November evening back in 2019 was one of the highlights of my life. Without her—and the inspiring Harris women, Maya and Meena—this book would not exist. Moreover, I am deeply grateful to the matriarch of this phenomenal family, Shyamala Gopalan Harris, whose frequent refrains "Do something about it and don't do it half-assed" and "We always show up excellent" have become my own mantras. As this book relied on previously published interviews and books, I'm incredibly grateful for the Harris family being forthcoming with the press, and for a free press whose reporting helped frame this book.

I'm deeply grateful for the Little, Brown Spark team for being the best partners on this project. Marisa Vigilante—thank you for entrusting this book to me, for your sharp edits, and for your kindness and support. Fanta Diallo—thank you for your patience with me in finalizing the details that turned this manuscript into a book. Scott Wilson—your edits made this book shine. To Jessica Chun, Juliana Horbachevsky, and Lauren Ortiz—thank you for getting this book out everywhere and anywhere and for sharing my own story. I couldn't have asked for a better team to work with.

I couldn't have done this without my own team. Kim Perel has my endless gratitude, admiration, and love as the greatest literary agent in the world. Kelly Lasserre and Tracie Ching's artwork brought this book to life. Austin Munhofen, Taber Stockstill, and LeVincia Porch held the various work forts as I buckled down to write this book, and they helped strategize its launch. Your check-ins and supportive messages mean more than I can put into words, and I'm so lucky to work with you all. My Skai Blue Media team—Christanna Ciabattoni, Leah Sinderbrand, Sabine Lavache—you are a dream to work with and masters of your craft. Thank you for getting *We're Speaking* on the shelves and in the hands of so many outlets I admire. My Rhoshan Pharmaceuticals team—Kevin O'Neill, Allan Clarke, Dean Kessler, Kathy Gans-Brangs—I can't thank you enough for your support and leadership while I all but disappeared for two months to write this book. We miss you dearly, Krish Venkat.

I also have to thank Sandra Joshel, Raymond Jonas, and Carl Bergstrom, my favorite history professors at the University of Washington. Everything I learned from them—how to research, how to evaluate data critically, to structure an argument, to write persuasively—is how I wrote this book.

It's my deepest honor to share the wisdom of so many women I admire in the pages of this book. Esther Ayorinde, Mandana Dayani, Komal Minhas, Rachel Cantor, Naj Austin, Rakia Reynolds, Marisa Renee Lee, Kat Cole, and Samira Panah Bakhtiar—thank you for your friendship and lending your words in this book. My deepest thanks to Ruchika Tulshyan, Minda Harts, Laura Venderkam, Nathalie Molina Niño, Casper ter Kuile, Elizabeth Holmes, Anjali Kumar, Susan McPherson, Grace Atwood, Melanie Notkin, and Eve Rodsky for your words and the work you do to help us all stand a little bit taller and stronger. Leah Fink, Jamie Kolnick, Neha Ruch, and Paula Herrera— thank you for keeping me sane and connected. Our group texts and little outings were the joyful moments I value so very much. Divya Gugnani, Alisha Kumar, Lisa Rubin, Janna Meyrowitz Turner, Fran Hauser,

Ashley Spivey, Morgan Hoit, Kimmery Martin, Allison Winn Scotch, Caroline Moss, Lupita Aquino, Jummy Olabanji, Arianna Afsar, Amanda Goetz, Becca Freeman, Lydia Hirt, Rachael King, Julia Lynch, Carmen Meyer, Kristin Kumar, Komal Mehta—your friendship and support mean the world to me, and I'm so grateful to have you in my corner. To my online community—your support means everything to me. Without your engagement, messages, and incredible questions every Q&A Friday, my corner of the Internet would be much lonelier and quieter. Thank you for being my friend, and for lifting me and my work up. It wouldn't exist without you.

Writing a book is not a solo endeavor, despite how it feels in the moment. Writing a book in two and a half months meant I had to drop most of my balls, and my family picked them up in my absence. Sri Narasimhan—you are the most incredible husband and father and I can't believe I get to grow old with you. You caught all the balls I had to drop in order to write this book, and juggled them perfectly. Rho and Rhaki—I'm so proud to be your mom, and your cuddles and hugs keep me going through all the hard things. I love you all across space-time. And to the friends that feel like family—Anu & Bharani Rajakumar, Girish and Kirti Tewani,

Sushma Dwivedi and Vivek Jindal—thank you for always being there for us.

To Naleeni Gangapersaud and Jeanne de Jesus—thank you for loving and caring for my sons and us the way you have. I could not have done it without you both. To my second parents Nara and Geetha Narasimhan, thank you for raising such incredible sons and for dropping everything to help out whenever we have needed you (and we really needed you while I wrote this book). While the book is focused on Vice President Harris, it also shares my own family's story. To Ram Palepu and Shanti Veluri—thank you for being the first (but not the last) Palepus to uproot your lives in India in pursuit of greater opportunities. While I'm an only child, I never felt alone because of my cousins and their kids. Bob and Jessica, thank you for your life-changing advice. Rav and Sailui, thank you for always being there. Bobby, Cahlin, Yagnik—thank you for preparing me for boy mom life. Neela—I miss you every single day. To all my other cousins and nieces and nephews—I love you all from the bottom of my heart.

And finally, to my parents, Nagesh and Bharathy Palepu. What can I even say? I don't know what things I did right in my previous lives to be born your daughter. Mom—you told me to go win the world when I was younger. I would rather be exactly like you and Dad instead. I could write another book about all the things I admire about you, but your refusal to put up with nonsense is the one quality that has helped me endure the past two years. You are strength, power, and beauty defined. Dad—you and Mom are the reason I've accomplished everything that I have. This book, our company, my ability to quote *The Godfather* on demand. You set out to create life-saving drugs and to be a good father, and you exceeded on both fronts. You both have modeled the kind of marriage and family life I wanted for myself and that Sri, the boys, and I enjoy today. *Thank you* feels inadequate for the gratitude and love I feel for you, but it's a start.

Bibliography

Chapter 1: Your Name and Your Multitudes Are Your Power

Roy, Keya, Zuheera Ali, and Medha Kumar. "The Racist Practice of Mispronouncing Names," *National Public Radio*, March 21, 2019.

Tulshyan, Ruchika. "If You Don't Know How To Say Someone's Name, Just Ask," *Harvard Business Review*, January 9, 2020.

Chapter 2: Do Something About It—And Don't Do It Half-Assed

Abrams, Stacey. "3 Questions to Ask Yourself About Everything," TED Video, November 2018.

Bilefsky, Dan. "In Canada, Kamala Harris, A Disco-Dancing Teenager, Yearned for Home," *The New York Times*, October 5, 2020.

Harris, Kamala. *The Truths We Hold*, New York: Penguin Books, 2019.

—. Twitter video, September 23, 2020.

Peritz, Ingrid. "How a Canadian Friend's Crisis Helped Shape Kamala Harris," *The Globe and Mail*, January 18, 2020.

Soul, Scott. "Where Kamala Harris' Political Imagination Was Formed," *Berkeley Blog*, September 25, 2020.

Chapter 3: Acting on Your Ambition

Chambers, Veronica. "Stacey Abrams Is 10 Steps Ahead of You (Isn't That Great?)," *Bustle*, August 27, 2019.

Flegenheimer, Matt. "Kamala Harris Was Ready to Brawl from the Beginning," *The New York Times,* September 15, 2019.

Harts, Minda. *The Memo: What Women of Color Need to Know to Secure a Seat at the Table,* New York: Basic Books, 2019.

Kruse, Michael. "How San Francisco's Wealthiest Families Launched Kamala Harris," *Politico Magazine,* August 9, 2019.

Morain, Dan. "2 More Brown Associates Get Well-Paid Posts: Government: The Speaker Appoints His Frequent Companion and a Longtime Friend to State Boards as His Hold on His Own Powerful Position Wanes," *Los Angeles Times,* November 29, 1994.

Pepitone, Julianne. "Stacey Abrams to Women: Don't Let Others Disqualify Your Ambition," NBC News, April 5, 2019.

Soltau, Alison. "Harris Toots Own Horn," *The Examiner,* July 21, 2004.

Wilentz, Amy. "Kamala Harris Is the Latest Product of San Francisco's Long-Running Political Machine," *Town and Country,* October 6, 2020.

Chapter 4: Focus on Your North Star

Borges, Anna. "13 Small but Impactful Ways to Cultivate Resilience," *Self,* May 28, 2020.

Cadelago, Christopher. "How Kamala Harris Seized the Moment on Race and Police Reform," *Politico,* June 7, 2020.

Collins, Denise. "Attorney General Kamala D. Harris Convenes Roundtable with Foreclosure Victims," California Department of Justice, November 9, 2011.

Davis, Amber and Tiffany Davis. "Purpose First, Tasks Second: Tips from Work-Life Changemaker Tiffany Dufu," *Forbes,* May 21, 2018.

Diaz, John. "Harris and the Death Penalty: Years of Consistency—And Conflict," *San Francisco Chronicle,* March 18, 2019.

Dweck, Carol. *Mindset: The New Psychology of Success,* New York: Random House, 2006.

—. "What Having a 'Growth Mindset' Actually Means," *Harvard Business Review,* January 13, 2016.

Harris, Kamala. "S.1593—115th Congress (2017–2018): Pretrial Integrity and Safety Act of 2017," bill introduced by Senate, July 20, 2017.

—. "Sen. Kamala Harris Presidential Campaign Announcement," C-SPAN, January 28, 2019.

—. "Transcript: Kamala Harris Kicks Off Presidential Campaign in Oakland," Fox KTVU, January 27, 2019.

—. *The Truths We Hold,* New York: Penguin Books, 2019.

—. Twitter video, November 1, 2020.

Harris, Shyamala G., Obituary, *San Francisco Chronicle,* March 22, 2009.

Hauck, Grace. "You're Facing a Lot of Choices Amid the Pandemic. Cut Yourself Slack: It's Called Decision Fatigue," *USA Today,* August 30, 2020.

Johnson, Chris. "Harris Takes 'Full Responsibility' for Briefs Against Surgery for Trans Inmates," *Washington Blade,* January 21, 2019.

King, Jamilah. "The Secret to Understanding Kamala Harris," *Mother Jones,* January/February 2018.

Kopan, Tal. "Kamala Harris Shaped by Berkeley and a 'Do Something' Mother," *San Francisco Chronicle,* August 16, 2020.

Lagos, Marisa. "Cooley, Harris Debate Packs Few Surprises but Good Discussion," *SFGate,* October 5, 2010.

Lazo, Alejandro. "Foreclosures Decline in California in 2010," *Los Angeles Times,* January 13, 2011.

Leonard, Jack and Seema Mehta. "Steve Cooley Concedes Race for Attorney General to Kamala Harris," *Los Angeles Times,* November 25, 2010.

Loewentheil, Kara. "Talking to Yourself," *Unf*ck Your Brain,* June 6, 2019.

Mason, Melanie and Michael Finnegan. "Kamala Harris Regrets California Truancy Law That Led to Arrest of Some Parents," *Los Angeles Times,* April 17, 2019.

Press release, "Senators Scott, Booker, Harris Lead Unanimous Passage of Federal Anti-Lynching Legislation | US Senator Tim Scott of South Carolina," February 14, 2019.

Seymour, Lesley Jane. "Say No to Work Life Balance," *Covey Club,* N.D.

Stannard, Matthew B. "San Francisco / DA Won't Pursue Death in Cop Slaying / Harris Fulfills Campaign Pledge with Decision," *SFGate,* April 14, 2004.

Tucker, Jill. "Pressuring Parents Helps S.F. Slash Truancy 23%," *San Francisco Chronicle,* June 9, 2009.

Van Derbeken, Jaxon. "Trials and Tribulations of Kamala Harris, DA / 2 Years Into Term, Prosecutor, Police Have Their Differences," *San Francisco Chronicle,* March 20, 2016.

Wondery. "For the Prosecution," *Kamala: Next in Line,* podcast.

Yam, Kimmy. "Overlooked 'Because of Her Accent': How the Story of Kamala Harris' Mom Resonates with Immigrants," NBC News, August 18, 2020.

Yoshino, Kimi. "Did Pension Comments Hurt Steve Cooley in L.A.?," *L.A. Now,* November 3, 2010.

Chapter 5: Eat No for Breakfast (And Take Care of Yourself)

Drinkard, Jane Starr. "Meena Harris Would Like to (Politely) Remind You That She Is 'Not Kamala'" *The Cut,* January 18, 2021.

Harris, Kamala. Instagram, April 23, 2020.

—. Instagram Live, May 1, 2020.

—. Twitter video, November 1, 2020.

Hauck, Grace. "You're Facing a Lot of Choices Amid the Pandemic. Cut Yourself Slack: It's Called Decision Fatigue," *USA Today,* August 30, 2020.

Kahn, Mattie. "What's Cooking, Kamala Harris?" *Glamour,* May 21, 2020.

Saujani, Reshma. *Brave, Not Perfect,* New York: Currency, 2019.

St. Flix, Doreen. "The Lenny Interview: Kamala Harris, the Senate Hopeful, Going after Revenge Porn," *Elle,* October 23, 2015.

ter Kuile, Casper. *The Power of Ritual: Turning Everyday Activities into Soulful Practices.* New York: HarperOne, 2020. 187.

Zuckerberg, Randi. *Pick Three: You Can Have It All (Just Not Every Day),* New York: Dey Street, 2018.

Chapter 6: Own Your Voice and Style

Borrelli-Persson, Laird. "Parsing the Meaning Behind Kamala Harris's Democratic Vice-Presidential Nomination Suit," *Vogue,* August 20, 2020.

Harris, Kamala. Speech, Spelman College, October 26, 2018.

Meraji, Shereen Marisol. "Let's Talk About Kamala Harris," National Public Radio, October 14, 2020.

Sedensky, Matt. "For Harris, Memories of Mother Guide Bid for Vice President," Associated Press, August 14, 2020.

St. Flix, Doreen. "The Lenny Interview: Kamala Harris, the Senate Hopeful, Going after Revenge Porn," *Elle,* October 23, 2015.

Vincent, Alice. "Obama's Secret Writing Weapon: What Is It About the Yellow Legal Pad?" Penguin, November 24, 2020.

Chapter 7: Lean on Your Family

Bolick, Kate. "Let's Hear It for Aunthood," *The New York Times,* September 16, 2011.

Harris, Kamala. Instagram, December 6, 2018.

——. "Watch Kamala Harris' VP Acceptance Speech: Full Transcript," *The New York Times,* November 8, 2020.

Munaweera, Nayomi. "What Kamala Harris Means to Women Who Are Childfree by Choice," *Vox,* January 26, 2021.

Perschbacher, Emily. "Super Aunts: Some Are Delaying Motherhood, Some Are Just Wild About Their Nieces and Nephews," *Chicago Tribune,* May 21, 2018.

richauntiesupreme. Instagram account.

Sedensky, Matt. "For Harris, Memories of a Warrior Mother Guide Her Campaign," Associated Press, May 11, 2019.

Chapter 8: Wait for Your Doug

Bennett, Jessica. "What's It Like to Have Kamala Harris as 'Momala'? We Asked Her Stepkids," *The New York Times,* January 17, 2021.

Gibbs, Karen. "Karen Gibbs on Her Best Friend Vice President Kamala Harris," *NewsTalk,* January 21, 2021.

Goldstein, Jessica. "Doug Emhoff on Kamala Harris, in His Own Words," *Marie Claire,* October 5, 2020.

Ho, Vivian. "'Nobody Works Harder': Insiders Recall Kamala Harris's Meteoric Rise," *The Guardian,* January 21, 2019.

"'Same Kamala': Harris' Friends Say Vice President Has Always Been Fearless," CBS News, January 21, 2021.

Wright, Jasmine and Veronica Stracqualursi. "Harris and Emhoff Recall First Date: 'It Felt Like We Had Known Each Other Forever,'" *CNN Politics,* January 15, 2021.

Chapter 9: Don't Be the Last

Bishari, Nuala Sawyer. "A Flare in the Dark," *SF Weekly,* June 7, 2017.

Burns, Alexander, Jonathan Martin, and Katie Glueck. "How Joe Biden Chose Kamala Harris as VP," *The New York Times,* August 13, 2020.

Harris, Kamala. "Kamala Harris's historic Victory Speech in Full: 'You Chose Truth,'" *The Guardian,* YouTube, November 7, 2020.

King, Jamilah. "The Secret to Understanding Kamala Harris," *Mother Jones,* January/February 2018.

Lerer, Lisa and Sydney Ember. "Kamala Harris Makes History as First Woman and Woman of Color as Vice President," *The New York Times,* November 7, 2020.

Molina Niño, Nathalie. Interview with author, January 18, 2021.

About the Author

Hitha Palepu is a woman of multitudes—a feminist, a lifelong politics enthusiast, a daughter of immigrants, and a mother raising feminist sons. These multitudes spill into her multihyphenate career as an entrepreneur, investor, writer, and speaker. Hitha's passion for the news and politics is captured in #5SmartReads, a Webby-honored social series that shares five must-read articles every day to keep her community informed without being overwhelmed. Hitha's longtime blog, Hitha on the Go, established her as an authority on lifestyle topics and paved the way to her book and collaborations with leading brands such as Headspace, Google, and Northwestern Mutual. Her book *How to Pack* was published by Clarkson Potter in 2017. As CEO of Rhoshan Pharmaceuticals, Hitha oversees financing, partnerships, and strategy for the company. Hitha also puts her money where her values are through early stage investing. A partner in Adama Ventures, she has invested in more than fifteen innovative companies primarily founded by and focused on women. She is a sought-after speaker on politics and the news, investing, entrepreneurship, work–life juggle, and motherhood. Hitha lives in New York with her husband and two sons.